THE
FULLNESS
OF
JOY

THE
FULLNESS
OF
JOY

CHARLES SPURGEON

Ⓦ *Whitaker House*

All Scripture quotations are taken from the *King James Version* (KJV) of the Holy Bible.

THE FULLNESS OF JOY

ISBN: 0-88368-412-8
Printed in the United States of America
Copyright © 1997 by Whitaker House

Whitaker House
30 Hunt Valley Circle
New Kensington, PA 15068

Library of Congress Cataloging-in-Publication Data

Spurgeon, C. H. (Charles Haddon), 1834–1892.
    The fullness of joy / Charles H. Spurgeon.
        p.   cm.
    ISBN 0-88368-412-8 (pbk.)
    1. Gratitude—Religious aspects—Christianity. 2. Joy—Religious
aspects—Christianity. 3. Praise of God. I. Title.
BV4647.G8S79   1997
241'.4—dc21   97-34323

3 4 5 6 7 8 9 10 11 12 / 07 06 05 04 03 02 01 00

Contents

Chapter One

Special Thanksgiving to the Father

*Giving thanks unto the Father, which hath made us
meet to be partakers of the inheritance of the saints
in light: who hath delivered us from the power
of darkness, and hath translated us
into the kingdom of his dear Son.*
—Colossians 1:12–13

Our first text is a mine of riches. I anticipate the difficulty I may experience in expressing the depths of these verses and the regret I may feel in concluding this chapter because I am not able to dig out all the gold that lies in this precious vein. I admit that I lack the power to truly grasp, as well as the ability to present, the volume of truths that has been condensed into these few sentences.

We are exhorted to give *"thanks unto the Father."* This counsel is simultaneously needed and advantageous for each and every one of us.

My friends, I think we scarcely need to be told to give thanks to the Son. The remembrance of His bleeding body hanging upon the cross is ever present to our faith. The nails and the spear, His griefs, the anguish of His soul, and His agonizing sweat make such tender, touching appeals to our gratitude that they will always prevent us from ceasing our songs and will often fire our hearts with rekindling rapture in praise of Christ Jesus. Yes, we will bless You, dearest Lord. Our souls are all on fire. As we survey the wondrous cross, we cannot but shout,

> O for this love let rocks and hills
> Their lasting silence break,
> And all harmonious human tongues
> The Savior's praises speak.

It is very much the same with the Holy Spirit. I think we are made to feel our dependence on His constant influence every day. He abides with us as a present, personal Comforter and Counselor. Thus, we praise the Spirit of Grace who has made our hearts His temple and who works in us all that is gracious, well-pleasing, and virtuous in the sight of God.

THE PRAISEWORTHY FATHER

If there is any one Person in the Trinity whom we are more apt to forget than the others in our praises, it is God the Father. In fact, some people even get a wrong idea of Him, a slanderous idea of our God whose name is Love. They imagine that love dwells in Christ, rather than in the Father, and that our salvation is due more to the Son and to the Holy Spirit, rather than to our Father God.

Let us not be numbered with the ignorant, but may we receive this truth for ourselves: we are as much indebted to God the Father as we are to any Person of the Sacred Three. Our heavenly Father loves us as much and as truly as any of the worthy Three Persons does. God the Father is as truly worthy of our highest praise as either the Son or the Holy Spirit is.

THE SOURCE OF GOD'S WORKS

A remarkable fact, which we should always bear in mind, is this: in the Scriptures most of the operations that are described as being the works of the Holy Spirit are ascribed to God the Father in other passages. Do we not say that God the Holy Spirit quickens (John 6:63) the sinner who is dead in sin? It is true, but you will find in another verse that it is said, *"The Father raiseth up the dead, and quickeneth them"* (John 5:21). Do we say that the Spirit is the Sanctifier and that the sanctification of the soul is a work of the Holy Spirit? Yes, but you will find a phrase in the opening of Jude's epistle in which he wrote, *"To them that are sanctified by God the Father"* (Jude 1:1).

Now, how are we to account for this? I think it may be explained this way. God the Spirit comes to us by the direction of God the Father. Therefore, whatever acts are performed by the Holy Spirit are truly done by the Father, because He sends forth the Spirit. The Spirit is often the instrument—although I do not say this in any way to detract from His glory—by which the Father works. It is the Father who says to the dry bones, *"live"* (Ezekiel 37:5); it is

9

the Spirit who, going forth with the divine word, makes them live. The quickening is due as much to the Father's word as to the Spirit's influence that went with the word. Since the word came with all the bounty of free grace and goodwill from the Father, the quickening is due to Him.

It is true that the Holy Spirit is the seal upon our hearts:

> *In whom ye also trusted, after that ye heard the word of truth, the gospel of your salvation: in whom also after that ye believed, ye were sealed with that holy Spirit of promise.* (Ephesians 1:13)

> *And grieve not the holy Spirit of God, whereby ye are sealed unto the day of redemption.*
> (Ephesians 4:30)

The Holy Spirit is the seal, but it is the Eternal Father's hand that stamps the seal. God the Father gives His Spirit to seal our adoption:

> *But when the Comforter is come, whom I will send unto you from the Father, even the Spirit of truth, which proceedeth from the Father, he shall testify of me.* (John 15:26)

> *Ye have received the Spirit of adoption, whereby we cry, Abba, Father.* (Romans 8:15)

I repeat, many of the works of the Spirit can ultimately be attributed to the Father because He works in, through, and by the Spirit.

I ought to make the observation here that the works of the Son of God are, every one of them, intimately connected with the Father. The Son came into the world because His Father sent Him. The

Son calls His people because His Father already gave them into His hands. When the Son redeemed the chosen race, was not the Son Himself the Father's gift? Did not God send His Son into the world so that we might live through Him? So then, the Father, the great Ancient of Days, is ever to be extolled; and we must never omit the full homage of our hearts to Him when we sing that sacred doxology:

Praise Father, Son, and Holy Ghost.

In order to stimulate your gratitude to God the Father, I want to discuss this glorious passage in Colossians in detail, as God enables me. If you look at the text, you will see two blessings in it. The first has to do with the present; it concerns our fitness to receive *"the inheritance of the saints in light."* The second blessing, which must go with the first, for indeed it is the effective cause of the first, is related to the past. Here we read of our deliverance from the power of darkness. Let us meditate a little upon each of these blessings. Then, I will endeavor to show the relationship that exists between the two.

A PRESENT BLESSING

The first blessing that comes to our notice is this: God the Father has qualified us as partakers of the inheritance of the saints in light. It is a present blessing. This is not one of the mercies laid up for us in the covenant that we have not yet received. Rather, it is a blessing that every true believer already has in his hand. Those future mercies in the covenant, of which we now have a down payment while we wait for their full possession, are just as

11

rich and just as certain as those that have already been bestowed on us with abundant lovingkindness. However, they still are not so precious in our enjoyment. The mercy we have in hand is, after all, the main source of our present comfort.

Already Qualified

Besides, what a blessing this is! *"Made...meet to be partakers of the inheritance of the saints in light."* The true believer is fit for heaven; he is qualified to be a partaker of the inheritance—and that is right now, at this very moment.

Does this mean that the believer is perfect, that he is free from sin? No, my friends, where could you ever find such perfection in this world? If no man but a perfect man could be a believer, then what would the perfect man have to believe? Could he not walk by sight? When he became perfect, he might cease to be a believer. No, it is not such perfection that is meant, although perfection is implied and assuredly will be given as the result.

In no way does this mean that we have a right to eternal life from any doings of our own. We have a fitness for eternal life, a suitability for it, but we have not earned it by our works. Even now, in ourselves we deserve nothing from God except His eternal wrath and His infinite displeasure.

The Bride to Be

What, then, does this phraseology mean? It means just this: we are so far qualified that we are *"accepted in the beloved"* (Ephesians 1:6), adopted into the family, and enabled by divine favor to dwell with the saints in light. For example, a woman is chosen to be a bride. She is qualified to be married and fit to enter into the honorable state and condition of matrimony, but at present she does not have on the bridal garment and is not like the bride adorned for her husband. You do not yet see her robed in her elegant attire and wearing her finest jewels, but you know she is fit to be a bride, because she has been received and welcomed as such into the family of her fiancé.

Likewise, Christ has chosen His church to be married to Him. She has not yet bathed herself and lain in the bed of spices for a little while. She has not yet put on her bridal garment and all the beautiful array in which she will stand before the Father's throne. Notwithstanding, however, there is a fitness in her to be the bride of Christ. There is such a fitness in her character, such a grace-given adaptation in her to become the royal bride of her glorious Lord and a partaker of the enjoyments of bliss, that it may be said of the church as a whole, and of every member of it, that they are *"meet to be partakers of the inheritance of the saints in light."*

Of Infants and Acorns

The original Greek word *hikanoo*, which was translated as *"meet,"* bears some of the meaning of suitability, although I cannot give the exact idiom. It is always difficult when a word is not used often. I am aware of this word being used only twice in the New Testament. The words *suitable, fit,* or *sufficient* may often be substituted for the word *meet.* God the

Father *"hath made us meet* [sufficient, suitable, worthy, fit] *to be partakers of the inheritance of the saints in light."*

I cannot express my idea of the meaning of this phrase without giving another illustration. When a child is born, it is at once endowed with all the faculties of humanity. If those powers are lacking at birth, they will not appear later on. The baby has eyes, hands, feet, and all its physical organs. Of course, these are rather undeveloped at birth. The senses, although perfect from the first, must be gradually refined, and the understanding gradually matured. The infant can see only a little; it cannot discern distances. The newborn can hear, but it cannot hear distinctly enough at first to know from what direction the sound comes. However, you never find a new leg, a new arm, a new eye, or a new ear growing on that child. Each of these powers will expand and enlarge, but still there is a complete person there at birth. Thus, the child is sufficiently equipped to become an adult. Let God in His infinite providence cause the infant to be nourished and give it strength and increase, and the babe has a sufficient, inherent ability to reach adulthood. It does not lack arm or leg, nose or ear—you cannot make it grow a new member—nor does it require a new member, either, because all are there.

In a similar manner, the moment a man is regenerated, there is every faculty in his new creation that there will be, even when he gets to heaven. His faculties only need to be developed and brought out. He will not gain a new power; he will not get a new grace. Rather, those abilities that he had previously will be developed and brought out.

Special Thanksgiving to the Father

We are told by the careful botanist that in an acorn there is every root and every bough and every leaf of the future tree in embryo, which only require being developed and brought out in their fullness as the parts of an oak tree. Similarly, in the true believer, there is a sufficiency or meetness *"to be partakers of the inheritance of the saints in light."* The believer does not require that a new thing be implanted in him, but rather that what God has instilled in the moment of regeneration would be cherished and nurtured and made to grow and increase, until it comes unto perfection and he enters into *"the inheritance of the saints in light."* This is, as near as I can give it to you, the meaning and interpretation of the text, as I understand it.

Equipped by the Father

However, you may ask me, "In what sense is this fitness for eternal life the work of God the Father? Have we already been made meet for heaven? How is this the Father's work?" Looking at the text, I will answer you in three ways: First, what is heaven? We read that it is an inheritance. Secondly, who are fit for an inheritance? Sons are. *"If a son, then an heir"* (Galatians 4:7). Thirdly, who makes us sons? God the Father does. *"Behold, what manner of love the Father hath bestowed upon us, that we should be called the sons of God"* (1 John 3:1).

A son has the capacity for an inheritance. The moment the son is born, he is qualified to be an heir. All that is needed is for him to grow up and be able to manage the possession. However, he is fit for an inheritance from the first. If he were not a son, he could not inherit as an heir. Now, as soon as we become sons of God, we are suited to inherit. There is in us the capacity, the power, and the potential to have an inheritance. The prerogative of the Father is to adopt us into His family.

> *Blessed be the God and Father of our Lord Jesus Christ, which according to his abundant mercy hath begotten us again unto a lively hope by the resurrection of Jesus Christ from the dead, to an inheritance incorruptible, and undefiled, and that fadeth not away, reserved in heaven for you.*
> (1 Peter 1:3–4)

Do you not see that, since being adopted is really the meetness for inheritance, it is the Father who has made us *"meet to be partakers of the inheritance of the saints in light"*?

Sanctified by the Father to Inherit

Heaven is an inheritance, but whose inheritance is it? It is an inheritance of the saints. It is not an inheritance of sinners, but of saints—that is, of the holy ones—of those who have been made saints by being sanctified. Turn to the Epistle of Jude, and you will see at once who it is that sanctifies. You will observe the moment you fix your eyes upon the passage that it is God the Father. In the first verse you read, *"Jude, the servant of Jesus Christ, and brother of James, to them that are sanctified by God the Father"* (Jude 1:1).

It is an inheritance for saints, and who are saints? The moment a man believes in Christ, he may know himself to have been truly set apart by

16

the covenant decree. He finds this consecration, if I
may use that word, verified in his own experience,
for he has now become *"a new creature"* (2 Corinthians 5:17) in Christ Jesus, separated from the rest of
the world. Then it is manifest and made known that
God has taken him to be His son forever.

The meetness that I must have, in order to enjoy
the inheritance of the saints in light, is my becoming
a son. God has made me and all believers sons;
therefore, we are meet for the inheritance. So then,
that meetness has come from the Father. Therefore,
how justly the Father claims and deserves our gratitude, our adoration, and our love!

From the Father of Lights

You will observe, however, it is not merely said
that heaven is the inheritance of the saints, but that
it is the inheritance of the saints *"in light."* So the
saints dwell in light—the light of knowledge, the
light of purity, the light of joy, the light of love, pure
ineffable love, the light of everything that is glorious
and ennobling. There they dwell, and if I am to appear fit for that inheritance, what evidence must I
have? I must have light shining into my own soul.

But, where can I get it? Do I not read that *"every
good gift and every perfect gift is from above, and
comes down"*? Yes, but from whom? From the Spirit?
No, *"from the Father of lights, with whom is no vari-
ableness, neither shadow of turning"* (James 1:17).
The preparation to enter into the inheritance in
light is light, which comes *"from the Father of lights."*
Therefore, my fitness, if I have light in myself, is the
work of the Father, and I must give Him praise.

QUALIFIED THREE WAYS

Do you see then, that as there are three nouns used here—*"the inheritance of the saints in light"*—so we have a threefold meetness? We are adopted and made sons so that we are qualified to inherit. God has sanctified us and set us apart. And then, He has put light into our hearts. All this is the work of the Father, and in this sense, we are *"meet to be partakers of the inheritance of the saints in light."*

Let me make a few general observations here. Beloved, I am persuaded that if an angel from heaven were to come right now and single out any one believer, there is not one believer who is unfit to be taken to heaven. You may not be ready to be taken to heaven at this time; by this I mean that, if I foresaw that you were going to live, I would tell you that you were in a certain sense unfit to die. But if you were to die now where you are, you are fit for heaven if you believe in Christ. You have a meetness even now that would take you there at once, without being committed to purgatory for a season. You are even now fit *"to be partakers of the inheritance of the saints in light."* You have but to gasp your last breath, and you would be in heaven. There would not be one spirit there more fit for heaven than you, nor one soul more adapted for the place than you are. You will be just as fitted for heaven's element as those who are nearest to the eternal throne.

This should make the heirs of glory think much of God the Father. When we reflect, my friends, on our state by nature and how fit we are to be firebrands in the flames of hell—yet to think that we are, at this very moment, if God Almighty willed it,

fit to sweep over the golden harpstrings with joyful
fingers, that our heads are fit this very night to wear
the everlasting crown, that our bodies are fit to be
girded with those fair white robes throughout eternity—I say, this makes us think gratefully of God
the Father. This makes us clap our hands with joy
and say, *"Thanks* [be] *unto the Father, which hath
made us meet to be partakers of the inheritance of the
saints in light."*

Do you not remember the penitent thief? Just a
few minutes before his conversion, he had been
cursing Christ. I do not doubt that he had joined
with the other, for it is written, *"They that were crucified with him reviled him"* (Mark 15:32). Not one,
but both—they both reviled Him. And then, a gleam
of supernatural glory lit up the face of Christ, and
the thief saw and believed. *"Jesus said unto him,
Verily I say unto thee, To day* [though the sun is set-
ting] *shalt thou be with me in paradise"* (Luke
23:43). No long preparation was required, no swel-
tering in purifying fires.

It will be the same with us. We may have been
in Christ Jesus, to our own knowledge, only seven
days, or we may have been in Him for seven years or
seven decades—the date of our conversion makes no
difference in our fitness for heaven, in a certain
sense. It is true, indeed, that the longer we live, the
more grace we have tasted, the riper we are becoming, and the more fit we are to be housed in heaven.
However, that is a different sense of the word; that
quality is the meetness that the Holy Spirit gives. In
contrast, regarding the fitness God the Father gives,
I repeat that the tiny blade of corn, the tender
growth of gracious wheat that has just appeared

above the surface of conviction, is as fit to be carried up to heaven as the fully grown corn in the ear. The sanctification by which we are sanctified by God the Father is not progressive; it is complete at once. We are now adapted for heaven, now fitted for it; by and by we will be completely ready for it and will enter into the joy of our Lord (Matthew 25:21).

I might have entered more fully into this subject, but I am short of space. I am sure I have left some knots still tied, but you must untie them yourselves, if you can. Let me recommend that you untie them on your knees—the mysteries of the kingdom of God are studied best when you are in prayer.

A PAST MERCY

The second mercy is mercy that looks backward. We sometimes prefer the mercies that look forward, because they unfold such a bright prospect: "Sweet fields beyond the swelling flood."

However, here is a mercy that looks backward. It turns its back, as it were, on the heaven of our anticipation and looks back on the gloomy past and the dangers from which we have escaped. Let us read the account of it: *"Who hath delivered us from the power of darkness, and hath translated us into the kingdom of his dear Son."* This verse is an explanation of the preceding one, as I will show you shortly. But just now let us survey this mercy by itself.

Under the Power of Darkness

My friends, what a description we have here of the manner of men we used to be! We were under *"the power of darkness."* Since I have been musing on this text, I have turned these words over and over in my mind: *"the power of darkness."* It seems to me one of the most awful expressions that man ever attempted to expound. I think I could deliver a discourse about it, if the Holy Spirit helped me, which might make every bone in your body shake.

"The power of darkness!" We all know that a moral darkness weaves its awful spell over the mind of the sinner. Where God is unacknowledged, the mind is void of judgment. Where God is not worshipped, the heart of man becomes a ruin. The chambers of that dilapidated heart are haunted by ghostly fears and degrading superstitions. The dark places of the reprobate mind are tenanted by vile lusts and noxious passions, like vermin and reptiles, from which we turn with disgust in open daylight.

Even the force of natural darkness is tremendous. With the solitary confinement that is practiced in some of our penitentiaries, the very worst results are produced if the treatment is prolonged.

If one of you were to be taken right now, led into some dark cavern, and left there, I can imagine that, for a moment, not knowing your fate, you might feel a childlike kind of interest about it. There might be, perhaps, a laugh as you found yourself in the dark. There might, from the novelty of the surroundings, be some momentary kind of curiosity excited. You might even feel a flush of silly joy.

In a little time you might endeavor to compose yourself to rest. Possibly you would even go to sleep. But, if you should awake and still find yourself down deep in the bowels of earth, where never a ray of sun or candle light could reach you, do you know the next feeling that would come over you? It would be a kind of idiotic thoughtlessness. You would find it impossible to control your desperate imagination; your heart would say, "O God, I am alone, so terribly alone, in this dark place." How you would look frantically all around! Since you would never catch a glimmer of light, your mind would begin to fail. Your next stage would be one of increasing terror. You would fancy that you saw something, and then you would cry, "If only I could see something, anything, whether friend or foe!" You would feel the dark sides of your dungeon. You would begin to scratch and scribble on the walls, as David did before king Achish (1 Samuel 21:13). Agitation would seize you.

If you were kept there much longer, delirium and death would be the consequence. We have heard of many who have been taken from the penitentiary to the lunatic asylum. The lunacy is produced partly by the solitary confinement and partly by the darkness in which they are placed. In a recent report written by the chaplain of Newgate Prison, there are some striking observations about the influence of darkness as a method of discipline. Its first effect is to shut the culprit up with his own reflections and make him realize his true position in the iron grasp of the outraged law. I think the defiant man, who has come in cursing and swearing, when he has found himself alone in darkness, where he cannot even hear the sound of passing traffic from the streets and can see no light whatsoever, is quickly subdued. He gives in and grows tame.

"The power of darkness" literally is something awful. If I had time, I would enlarge upon this subject. We cannot properly describe what *"the power of*

darkness" is, even in this world. The sinner is plunged into the darkness of his sins, and he sees nothing, he knows nothing. Let him remain there a little longer, and his joy of curiosity—the hectic joy that he now has in the path of sin—will die away. A spirit of slumber will then come over him. Sin will make him drowsy, so that he will not hear the voice of the Spirit, crying to him to escape for his life. Let him continue in his life of sin, and by and by it will make him spiritually an idiot. He will become so set in sin that common reason would be lost on him. All the arguments that a sensible man could receive would only be wasted on him. Let him go on, and he will proceed from bad to worse, until he acquires the raving mania of a desperado in sin. Let death step in, and the darkness will have produced its full effect: he will come into the delirious madness of hell. Only the power of sin is needed to make a man more truly hideous than human thought can realize or language can express. Oh, *"the power of darkness!"*

Now my friends, all of us were under this power once. It is but a few months or years—a few weeks with some of you—since you were under the power of darkness and of sin. Some of you had only gotten as far as the curiosity of sin; others had gone as far as the sleepiness stage; a good many of you had gone as far as the apathy of it; and some of you may have been almost caught up in the terror of it. You had so cursed and sworn, you had so yelled out your blasphemies, that you seemed to be ripening for hell. But, praised and blessed be the name of the Father, He has *"delivered* [you] *from the power of darkness, and hath translated* [you] *into the kingdom of his dear Son."*

23

The Fullness of Joy

Translated by the Father

Having thus explained this term *"the power of darkness"* to show you what you were, I want to examine the next phrase, *"and hath translated us."* What a unique word this *translated* is. You probably think it means the process by which a word is interpreted to retain the original meaning when the expression is rendered in another language. That is one meaning of the word *translation*, but it is not the meaning here. The word is used by Paul in this sense: the taking away of a people who have been dwelling in a certain country and planting them in another place. This is called *translation*. We sometimes hear of a bishop being translated or transferred from one jurisdiction or district to another.

Now, if you would like to have this concept explained, let me give you an overview of an amazing instance of a great translation. The children of Israel were in Egypt under taskmasters who oppressed them very severely and brought them into iron bondage. What did God do for these people? There were over two million of them. He did not temper the tyranny of the tyrant; He did not influence the pharaoh's mind to give them a little more liberty. Instead, God translated His people. With a high hand and an outstretched arm, He took every one of His chosen men, women, and children bodily out of Egypt, led them through the wilderness, and translated them into the kingdom of Canaan, where they were settled. What an achievement that was! With their flocks and their herds and their little ones, the whole host of Israel went out of Egypt, crossed the Jordan, and came into Canaan!

Special Thanksgiving to the Father

My dear friends, the whole of the Exodus was not equal to the achievement of God's powerful grace when He brings one poor sinner out of the region of sin into the kingdom of holiness and peace. I believe it was easier for God to bring Israel out of Egypt, to split the Red Sea, to make a highway through the pathless wilderness, to drop manna from heaven, to drive out the giant inhabitants—it was easier for Omnipotence to do all this than to translate a man *"from the power of darkness...into the kingdom of his dear Son."* This is the grandest achievement of God Almighty.

I believe that the sustenance of the whole universe is even easier than the changing of a bad heart and the subduing of an iron will. But, thanks be to the Father, He has done all that for you and for me. He has brought us out of darkness. He has translated us by taking up the old tree, which had struck its roots ever so deep—taking it up roots and all—and then planting it in good soil. He had to cut the top off, it is true—the high branches of our pride—but the tree has grown better in the new soil than it ever did before. Who ever heard of transplanting as huge a tree as a man who has grown for fifty years in sin?

Oh, what wonders our Father has done for us! He has taken the wild leopard, tamed it into a lamb, and purged away its spots. He has regenerated the poor sinner—oh, how black we were by nature! Our blackness permeated our beings to the center of our hearts. But, blessed be His name, He has washed us white and is still carrying on the divine operation, and He will yet completely deliver us from every taint of sin and will finally bring us *"into the kingdom of his dear Son."* Here then, in this second mercy, we discern from what and how we were delivered—God the Father has *"translated us."*

Into the Kingdom

But where are we now? Into what place is the believer brought when he is brought out from under the power of darkness? He is brought into the kingdom of God's dear Son. Into what other kingdom would a Christian desire to be brought? Friends, a republic may sound very good in theory, but in spiritual matters, the last thing we want is a republic.

We need a kingdom. I love to have Christ as the absolute Monarch in my heart. I do not want to have a doubt about it. I want to give up all my liberty to Him, because I feel that I will never be free until I abdicate the throne to Him, and that I will never have my will truly free until it is bound in the golden fetters of His sweet love. We are brought into a kingdom where Christ is Lord and Sovereign. He has *"made us kings and priests unto God"* (Revelation 1:6), and we *"shall reign with him"* (Revelation 20:6).

The proof that we are in this kingdom must consist in our obedience to our King. Here, perhaps, we may raise many causes and questions, but surely we can say that, although we have offended our King many times, yet our hearts are loyal to Him after all. "Oh, precious Jesus, we would obey You and yield submission to every one of Your laws; our sins are not willful or beloved sins. Although we fall, we can truly say that we want to be holy as You are holy; our hearts are true toward Your statutes. Lord, help us to *'run the way of thy commandments'*" (Psalm 119:32).

Thus, you see, this mercy that God the Father has given to us, this second of these present mercies, is that He has *"translated us into the kingdom of his dear Son."* This is the Father's work. Will we not love God the Father from this day forth? Will we not give Him thanks, sing our hymns to Him, exalt His great name, and triumph in His merciful love?

MAKING THE CONNECTION

Now, I would like to show you how these two verses relate to each other. When I get a passage of Scripture to meditate upon, I like, if I can, to see its overall meaning. Then I like to examine its various parts to see if I can understand each one separately, and then I go back again to see what one clause has to do with another. I repeatedly looked at this text and wondered what connection there could be between the two verses. *"Giving thanks unto the Father, which hath made us meet to be partakers of the inheritance of the saints in light."* Well, that is good. We can see how making us meet to go to heaven is the work of God the Father. But, does the next verse, *"Who hath delivered us from the power of darkness, and hath translated us into the kingdom of his dear Son,"* have anything to do with our fitness?

Well, I read it again, and I decided to view it this way. The twelfth verse tells me that the inheritance of heaven is the inheritance of light. Is not heaven light? Then I can see my fitness for it as described in the thirteenth verse: *"Who hath delivered* [me] *from the power of darkness."* Is that not the same thing? If I am delivered from the power of darkness, is that not being suited to dwell in the light? If I am now brought out of darkness into the light, and if I am walking in the light, is not that the very suitability which is spoken of in the verse before?

Then I continue to read. The Scripture says that we are saints. Well, saints are people who obey the Son. Here is my meetness then in the thirteenth verse, where it says, *"Who hath delivered us from the power of darkness, and hath translated us into the kingdom of his dear Son."* So, I not only have the light, but the sonship also, for I am in *"the kingdom of his dear Son."*

A Heavenly Inheritance

But, what about the inheritance? Is there anything about that in the thirteenth verse? The entire thing is an inheritance. Do I find anything about a fitness for it there? Yes, I find that I am in *"the kingdom of his dear Son."* How did Christ come to have a kingdom? Why, by inheritance. Then, it seems that I am in His inheritance; and if I am in His inheritance here, then I am fit to be in it above, for I am in it already. I am even now part of it and partner to it, since I am in the kingdom that He inherits from His Father. Therefore, there is the meetness.

I do not know whether I have expressed this plainly enough, so I will summarize. You see, heaven is a place of light. Our having been brought out of darkness is, of course, our meetness for light. Heaven is a place for sons. When we are brought into the kingdom of God's dear Son, we are adopted as sons, so that there is the meetness for it. Heaven is an inheritance. When we are brought into the inherited kingdom of God's dear Son, we enjoy the inheritance now and, consequently, are suited to enjoy it forever.

LIFE LESSONS

Having shown the connection between these verses, I want to make a few general observations. I like to explain the Scripture so that we can draw some practical inferences from it. I think I have stated some of these lessons many times already. I am repeating them so often so that we may never forget them. Martin Luther said that even though he preached upon justification by faith every day in the week, the people still would not understand. There are some truths, I believe, that need to be said over and over again, either because our silly hearts will not receive them or our treacherous memories will not hold them.

Praise the Father

Of course, the first inference we can draw from this Scripture is this: let us, from this time on, never omit God the Father in our praises. I implore you to habitually sing the praises of the Father in heaven, just as you do the praises of the Son hanging upon the cross. Love God, the eternal Father God, as truly as you love the God-man, Jesus, the Savior who once died for you. That is the greatest lesson.

Be Certain of Your Position in Christ

Yet another inference arises. Beloved, are you conscious that you are not now what you once were?

Are you sure that the power of darkness does not now rest upon you, that you love divine knowledge, that you are panting after heavenly joys? Are you sure that you have been *"translated...into the kingdom of* [God's] *dear Son"*?

If you can answer those questions in the affirmative with certainty, then you never need to be troubled about thoughts of death. Whenever death may come, you have been made ready to be a partaker *"of the inheritance of the saints in light."* Let no thought distress you about death's coming to you at an unseasonable hour. Should it come tomorrow, should it come now, if your "faith is fixed on nothing less than Jesus' blood and righteousness," you will see the face of God with acceptance.

I have the consciousness in my soul, by the witness of the Holy Spirit, of my adoption into the family of God. I feel that, even if I never preached again, but would lay down my body and my ministry before I could even reach my home and take my final rest in bed, *"I know that my redeemer liveth"* (Job 19:25), and that I would be a partaker *"of the inheritance of the saints in light."* It is not always that one feels this way. However, may you never be satisfied until you do, until you know your fitness for heaven; until you are conscious of it; until, moreover, you are longing to be gone, because you feel that you have powers that never can be satisfied short of heaven—powers that only heaven can employ.

Adapted for Your Eternal Abode

One more reflection lingers. Some of you cannot be thought, by the utmost charity of judgment, to be *"meet to be partakers of the inheritance of the saints in light."* If a wicked man should go to heaven without being converted, heaven would be no heaven to him. Heaven is not adapted for sinners. It is not a place for them.

If you were to take someone who has long lived near the equator up to where the Eskimos dwell, telling him that you would show him the aurora and all the glories of the North Pole, the poor wretch could not appreciate them. He would say, "It is not the element for me; it is not the place where I could be happy!" On the other hand, if you were to take some northern dweller down to a tropical region where trees grow to a stupendous height and where the spices give their balmy odors to the gale, and if you were to tell him to live there in that torrid zone, he could enjoy nothing. He would say, "This is not the place for me, because it is not adapted to my nature." Or, if you were to take a vulture, which has never fed on anything but carrion, put it into the noblest dwelling you could make for it, and feed it the daintiest meals, it would not survive because it is not adapted to that kind of food.

Likewise, you sinner, you are nothing but a carrion vulture. Nothing makes you happy but sin. You do not like too much hymn singing, do you? Sunday is a dull day for you. You want to have all the Sabbath activities over and done with. You do not care about your Bible. You would prefer that there were no Bible at all. You find that going to church is very dull work indeed. Oh, then, you will not be troubled with that in eternity, so do not agitate yourself. If you die as you are and do not love God, you will go to join your own company. You will be with your jolly mates, your good fellows. Those who have been your friends and companions on earth will be your mates forever.

Unless you repent and are converted, you will go to the domain of the Prince of those good fellows. Where God is, you cannot come. It is not an element suited to you. You might as well place a bird at the bottom of the sea, or put a fish in the air, as place an ungodly sinner in heaven.

How to Be Suited for Heaven

What is to be done then? You must have a new nature. I pray that God may give it to you. Remember, if you now feel your need of a Savior, that is the beginning of the new nature. *"Believe on the Lord Jesus Christ, and thou shalt be saved"* (Acts 16:31). Throw yourself totally on His mercy, trust in nothing but His blood, and then you will be filled with a new nature. You will be made ready by the Holy Spirit's operations to partake in *"the inheritance of the saints in light."*

Many a man has come into my church as a rollicking fellow, fearing neither God nor the Devil. Many a man has come from a bar and entered into our services. If he had died at that moment, where would his soul have been? Yet, the Lord met him as he walked through our doors. Many trophies of that grace are now in my congregation. They can say, *"Thanks [be] unto the Father,...who hath delivered us from the power of darkness, and hath translated us into the kingdom of his dear Son."*

If God has done that for some, why cannot He do it for others? O poor sinner, why do you need to despair? If you are the worst sinner outside of hell, remember, the gate of mercy stands wide open, and Jesus bids you to come in. Conscious of your guilt, flee. Flee to Him. Look to His cross, and you will find pardon in His veins and life in His death.

Chapter Two

Jesus, Our Example of Holy Praise

I will declare thy name unto my brethren:
in the midst of the congregation will I praise thee.
Ye that fear the LORD, praise him;
all ye the seed of Jacob, glorify him;
and fear him, all ye the seed of Israel.
—Psalm 22:22–23

We greatly esteem the dying words of good men, but what must be the value of their departing thoughts! If we could pass beyond the gate of speech and could see the secret things that are transacted in the silent chambers of their souls in the moment of departure, we might greatly value the revelation. There are thoughts that the tongue cannot and must not utter, and there are deep searchings of heart that cannot be expressed by syllables and sentences. If we could somehow read the innermost thoughts of holy men as they near death, we might be privileged indeed.

THE RULING PASSION OF JESUS

Now, in the Psalm before us and especially in the words of our text verses, we have the last thoughts of our Lord and Master. They beautifully illustrate the fact that He was governed by one ruling passion: that ruling passion, which was most strong in death, was the glorification of God. When Jesus was but a child, He declared, *"I must be about my Father's business"* (Luke 2:49). Throughout His ministry Jesus could have constantly said, *"The zeal of thine house hath eaten me up"* (John 2:17), and *"My meat is to do the will of him that sent me, and to finish his work"* (John 4:34). Then, at the last, as He expired, with His hands and His feet nailed to the cross and His body and soul in extreme anguish (Psalm 22:14–16), His one thought was that God would be glorified. In that last interval before He actually gave up His soul into His Father's hands, His thoughts rushed forward and found a blessed place of rest in the prospect that, as the result of His death, *"all the kindreds of the nations shall worship before thee"* (v. 27), and that the Most High should be honored by a chosen seed (v. 30).

May we have the same concentration upon one thing, and may that one thing be the glory of God! May we be able to say with Paul, *"This one thing I do"* (Philippians 3:13), and may this one thing be the chief end of our being—the glorifying of our Creator, our Redeemer, the Lord of our hearts!

My immediate objective is to arouse in you the spirit of adoring gratitude. Most of us see Christ as our example of how to pray, but I would like to exhibit Him to you as our model for grateful praising.

Then I want to ask you to follow Him as your leader in the delightful practice of magnifying the name of God Almighty.

> Far away be gloom and sadness;
>   Spirits with seraphic fire,
> Tongues with hymns, and hearts with gladness,
>   Higher sound the chords and higher.

In considering our text, we will begin with our Lord's example: *"I will declare thy name unto my brethren: in the midst of the congregation will I praise thee."* And then, we will examine our Lord's exhortation: *"Ye that fear the LORD, praise him; all ye the seed of Jacob, glorify him; and fear him, all ye the seed of Israel."*

CHRIST'S EXAMPLE IN DECLARING GOD'S NAME

The praise that Jesus as our Exemplar rendered unto the eternal Father was twofold. First, we have His praise of declaration, *"I will declare thy name unto my brethren,"* which is followed by His more direct and immediate thanksgiving, *"In the midst of the congregation will I praise thee."*

Through His Teaching

The first form of praise that our blessed Mediator rendered unto the eternal Father is that of declaring God's name. My dear friends, you know that Christ repeatedly did this in His teaching.

Some characteristics of God had been revealed to men throughout history. God had spoken to Noah and Abraham, Isaac and Jacob, and especially to His servant Moses. He had been pleased to display Himself in diverse types and ceremonies and ordinances. He was known as Elohim, El Shaddai, and Jehovah, among others. However, never until Christ came did men begin to say, *"Our Father which art in heaven"* (Matthew 6:9). This was the loving word by which the Well Beloved declared His Father's name unto the Israelites. The sterner attributes of God had been discovered amid the thunders of Sinai, the waves of the Red Sea, the smoke of Sodom, and the fury of the Deluge. The splendor of the Most High had been seen and wondered at by the prophets who spoke as they were moved by the Holy Spirit.

By Declaring God As Father

The full radiance of a Father's love, however, was never seen until it was beheld as it beamed through the Savior's face. Christ said, *"He that hath seen me hath seen the Father"* (John 14:9), but until they had seen the Son, they could not see God as Father. Jesus said, *"No man cometh unto the Father, but by me"* (John 14:6). Just as no man can come to God affectionately in the yearnings of his heart or credibly in the actions of his faith, so neither can any man come to God in the enlightenment of understanding except by Jesus Christ, the Son.

The person who understands Christianity has a far better idea of God than he who only comprehends Judaism. When you read the Old Testament through, you will value every sentence and prize it *"above fine gold"* (Psalm 119:127). Yet, you still will feel unrest and dissatisfaction, because the vision is veiled and the light is dim. Turn then to the New

Testament, and you discern that in Jesus of Nazareth *"dwelleth all the fulness of the Godhead bodily"* (Colossians 2:9). The bright light of knowledge is around you, and the vision is open and distinct. Jesus is the express image of His Father, and in seeing Him, you have seen God manifest in the flesh. You will assuredly see this sight of God if you are one of those to whom, through the Spirit, Jesus Christ declares the name of the Father.

By His Acts

Our Lord, however, revealed the Father perhaps more by His acts than by His words, for the life of Christ is a discovery of all the attributes of God in action. If you want to know the gentleness of God, perceive Jesus receiving sinners and eating with them. If you would like to know His condescension, behold the loving Redeemer taking little children into His arms and blessing them. If you want to know whether God is just, hear the words of the Savior as He denounces sin, and observe His own life: He *"is holy, harmless, undefiled, separate from sinners"* (Hebrews 7:26). Would you know the mercy of God as well as His justice? Then see it manifested in the thousand miracles of the Savior's hands and in the constant sympathy of the Redeemer's heart.

I cannot belabor this to bring out all the incidents in the Redeemer's life, nor even to give you a brief sketch of it. But, suffice it to say, the life of Christ is a perpetual unrolling of the great mystery of the divine attributes. Be assured that what Jesus is, so the Father is. You need not be startled by the Father, as though He were something strange and unrevealed. You have seen the Father if you have seen Christ. If you have studied well and taken the history of the Man of Sorrows deeply into your spirit, you understand, as well as you need to, the character of God over all, blessed forever.

In His Suffering

Our Lord made a grand declaration of the Godhead through His suffering.

> Here His whole name appears complete,
>   Nor wit can guess, nor reason trace,
> Which of the letters best is writ—
>   The power, the wisdom, or the grace.

There at Calvary, where Christ suffered—the just for the unjust—to bring us to God, we see the Godhead, resplendent in noonday majesty, although it seems to be eclipsed in midnight gloom to the natural eye. Do you desire to see the justice that the Righteous Judge perpetually exhibits? *"Shall not the Judge of all the earth do right?"* (Genesis 18:25). Would you see the kind of justice that will not spare the guilty, which smites at sin with determined enmity and will not endure it? Then, behold the hands and feet and side of the Redeemer, welling up with crimson blood! Behold His heart, broken as with an iron rod, dashed to slivers as though it were a potter's vessel! Hearken to His cries. Mark the lines of grief that mar His face. Behold the turmoil, the confusion, the whirlwinds of anguish that seethe like a boiling cauldron within the soul of the Redeemer! In all of these things, the vengeance of God is revealed to men, so that they may see it and not die, so that they may behold it and weep, but not with the tears of despair.

In His Death

Similarly, if you desire to see the grace of God, where else could you discover it as you do in the death of Jesus? God's bounty gleams in the light, flashes in the rain, and sparkles in the dew. It blossoms in the flowers that decorate the meadows, and it ripens in the golden sheaves of autumn. All of God's works are full of goodness and truth. The steps of the beneficent Creator are on the sea itself. Yet, all this does not meet the need of guilty, condemned man. Thus, to the eye of him who has wept for sin, nature does not reveal the goodness of God in a more glorious light than that which gleams from the cross.

God is seen best of all as He who *"spared not his own Son, but delivered him up for us all"* (Romans 8:32). *"Herein is love, not that we loved God, but that he loved us"* (1 John 4:10). *"God commendeth his love toward us, in that, while we were yet sinners, Christ died for us"* (Romans 5:8).

Your thoughtful minds will readily discover every one of the great qualities of deity in our dying Lord. You have only to linger long enough amid the wondrous scenes of Gethsemane and Gabbatha and Golgotha to observe how power and wisdom, grace and vengeance, strangely join.

> Piercing His Son with sharpest smart
> To make the purchased blessing mine.

Beloved, *"in the midst of the congregation,"* a dying Savior declares the name of the Lord, and thus

He magnifies the Lord as no other can. None of the harps of angels nor the fiery, flaming sonnets of cherubs can glorify God as did the wounds and pangs of the great Substitute when He died to make His Father's grace and justice known.

In His Resurrection

Our Lord continued to declare God's name among His people when He rose from the dead. He literally did so. Among the very first words He said were, *"Go to my brethren,"* and His message to them was, *"I ascend unto my Father, and your Father; and to my God, and your God"* (John 20:17). After His resurrection, Christ's life on earth was very brief, but it was very rich and instructive. In itself it was a showing forth of divine faithfulness.

Christ further revealed the faithfulness and glory of God *"when he ascended up on high,* [and] *led captivity captive"* (Ephesians 4:8). It must have been a magnificent day when the Son of God actually passed through the pearly gates to remain within the walls of heaven, enthroned until His Second Advent! How must *"the spirits of just men made perfect"* (Hebrews 12:23) have risen from their seats of bliss to gaze on Him! They had not seen a risen one before. Two had passed into heaven without death, but none had entered into glory as risen from the dead. He was the first instance of immortal resurrection, *"the firstfruits of them that slept"* (1 Corinthians 15:20). How angels adored Him! How holy beings wondered at Him while

> The God shone gracious through the man,
> And shed sweet glories on them all!

Jesus, Our Example of Holy Praise

Celestial spirits saw the Lord that day as they had never seen Him before! They had worshipped God, but the excessive brilliance of absolute Deity had forbidden the sacred familiarity with which they hailed the Lord as He was arrayed in flesh. They were never so near Deity before, for in the Son of Man the Godhead veiled its unapproachable splendor and wore the aspect of a fatherhood and brotherhood most near and dear. The magnificent whole was sweetly shrouded in humanity. Still, enough was seen of glory, as much as finite beings could bear, that God was declared in a new and more delightful manner, and heaven rang out with newborn joy.

In Heaven

What if I say that I think a part of the occupation of Christ in heaven is to declare to perfect spirits what He suffered and how God sustained Him; to reveal to them the covenant and all its solemn bonds, how the Lord ordained it, how He made it firm by His guarantee, and how He based it upon an eternal settlement, so that everlasting mercy might flow from it forever?

What if, contrary to popular opinion, there is preaching in heaven? What if Christ is the Preacher there, speaking as man never spoke before? What if He is forever instructing His saints that they may make known unto principalities and powers yet more fully the manifold wisdom of God as revealed truth in them and in Him—in them, the members, and in Him, the Head! I think that if it is so, it is a sweet fulfillment of this dying vow of our blessed Master, *"I will declare thy name unto my brethren."*

43

The Fullness of Joy

Through Spreading the Gospel

But, beloved, it is certain that at this time our Lord Jesus Christ continues to fulfill His vow by the spreading of His Gospel on earth. Do not tell me that the Gospel declares God, but that Jesus does not do so. I would remind you that the Gospel does not declare God apart from the presence of Jesus Christ with it. *"Lo, I am with you alway, even unto the end of the world"* (Matthew 28:20) is the Gospel's true life and power. If you take Christ's presence away, all the doctrines and precepts and the invitations of the Gospel would not declare God to this blind-eyed generation, this hard-hearted multitude. But, where Jesus is by His Spirit, there the Father is declared by the Word.

Moreover, my friends, this great process will go on. All through the present dispensation, Christ is declaring God to the sons of men, especially to the elect sons of men, His own family. Then will come the latter days of which we know so little, but of which we hope so much. In that noble period, there will be a declaration, no doubt, of God in brilliant light, for it will be said, *"The tabernacle of God is with men, and he will dwell with them"* (Revelation 21:3). Jesus will be the Sun of that age of light. The great Revealer of Deity will still be the Son of Mary, the Man of Nazareth, the *"Wonderful, Counsellor, the mighty God, the everlasting Father, the Prince of Peace"* (Isaiah 9:6). Each one of us will spread abroad the sweet sound of His name until He comes again. Then we will have no need to say to one another, *"Know the Lord: for all shall know [Him], from the least to the greatest"* (Hebrews 8:11). All will know the Lord for this reason: because they know Christ and have seen God in the person of Jesus Christ His Son.

Unto His Brethren

For both he that sanctifieth and they who are sanctified are all of one: for which cause he is not ashamed to call them brethren....Forasmuch then as the children are partakers of flesh and blood, he also himself likewise took part of the same.
(Hebrews 2:11, 14)

I cannot leave this passage without urging you to treasure that precious word of our Master: *"I will declare thy name unto my brethren."*

> Our next of kin, our brother now,
> Is He to whom the angels bow;
> They join with us to praise His name
> But we the nearest interest claim.

The Savior's brothers are all to know God in Christ. You who are one with Jesus, you who have been adopted into the same family, have been regenerated and quickened with His life. You who are joined together by an indissoluble union—you are to see the Lord. Yes, an indissoluble union, for a wife may be divorced from her husband, but there is no divorce of brothers. I never heard of any law, human or divine, that could ever unbrother a man; that cannot be done. If a man is my brother, he is now and will be my brother, even when heaven and earth pass away. Am I Jesus' brother? Then I am joint heir with Him (Romans 8:17). I share in all He has and all that God bestows upon Him: His Father is my

Father; His God is my God. Feast, my brothers and sisters, on this rich morsel, and go your way in the strength of it to bear the trials of earth with more than mere patience.

FOLLOWING CHRIST'S EXAMPLE

Our Lord's example, in this instance, I can only hint at. It is this: if the Lord Jesus Christ declares God, especially to His own brethren, it must be your business and mine to proclaim what we know of the excellence and surpassing glories of our God. In this way we may praise God Almighty. Especially let us speak of Him to our immediate families, our relatives, our neighbors, and—since all men are our brothers, in a sense—let us speak of the Father wherever we find ourselves. Dear friends, I truly desire that we talk more about our God.

> But, ah, how faint our praises rise!
> Sure 'tis the wonder of the skies,
> That we, who share His richest love,
> So cold and unconcerned should prove.

How many times this week have you praised the dear Redeemer to your friends? Have you done it once? I do it often officially as a pastor, but I wish I did it more often, spontaneously and personally, to those with whom I may come in contact. Undoubtedly, this week you have murmured and complained, spoken against your neighbors, spread abroad some small amount of scandal, or just talked carelessly and without integrity. It is even possible that impurity has been in your speech; even a Christian's language is not always as pure as it should be.

Oh, if we saved our breath to praise God, how much wiser we would be! If our mouths were filled with the Lord's praise and with His honor all the day, how much holier! If we would but speak of what Jesus has done for us, what good we might accomplish! Why, every man speaks of what he loves. Men can hardly hold their tongues about their inventions and their delights. Speak well, you faithful ones, of the Lord's name. I urge you, do not be silent concerning the One who deserves so much from you, but make this your resolve right now: *"I will declare thy name unto my brethren."*

A DIRECT MODEL OF PRAISE

Our Master's second form of praise in the text is of a more direct kind: *"In the midst of the congregation will I praise thee."* Is this just my imagination, or does the text really mean that the Lord Jesus Christ, as man, adores and worships the eternal God in heaven and is, in fact, the great Leader of the adoration in the skies? Would I err if I say that they all bow when He as Priest adores the Lord and that all join their voices with the lifting up of His sacred psalm? Is He the Chief Musician of the sky, the Master of the sacred choir? Does He beat time for all the hallelujahs of the universe? I think so. I think that is the meaning of these words: *"In the midst of the congregation will I praise thee."*

As God, Christ is and will be forever praised. Far above all worshipping, He Himself is forever worshipped. But as Man, the Head of redeemed humanity, the ever living Priest of the Most High God, I believe that He praises Jehovah in heaven. Surely it is the office of the Head to speak and to represent the holy joys and devout aspirations of the whole body that He represents.

"In the midst of the congregation[s]" of earth, too, is not Jesus Christ the sweetest of all singers? I like to think that when we pray on earth, our prayers are not alone, but our great High Priest is there to offer His own petitions with ours. When we sing on earth, it is the same. Is not Jesus Christ *"in the midst of the congregation,"* gathering up all the notes that come from sincere lips, to put them into the golden censer and to make them rise as precious incense before the throne of the infinite Majesty? Thus, He is the great Singer, rather than we. He is the chief Player on our stringed instruments, the great Master of true music. The worship of earth comes up to God through Him, and He is the accepted channel of all the praise of all the redeemed universe.

I am anticipating the day—I hope we are all longing for it—when *"the dead in Christ shall rise"* (1 Thessalonians 4:16), when the sea and land will give up the treasured bodies of the saints, when glorified spirits will descend to enliven their renovated frames, when *"we which are alive and remain"* (v. 17) will be changed and made immortal, and the King Himself will be revealed. Then, all the ashes of our enemies will be trodden under our feet; Satan, bound, will be held under the foot of Michael, the great archangel; and victory will be on the side of truth and righteousness.

What a "Hallelujah Chorus" will peal from land and sea and far-off islands: *"Alleluia: for the Lord God omnipotent reigneth"* (Revelation 19:6)! Who

will lead that song? Who will be the first to praise
God in that day of triumph? Who first will wave the
palm of victory? Who but He who was first in the
fight and first in the victory, He who trod the
winepress alone and stained His garments with the
blood of His enemies, He who *"cometh from Edom,
with dyed garments from Bozrah"* (Isaiah 63:1)?
Surely it is He who, in the midst of the exulting host,
once militant and then triumphant, will magnify and
adore Jehovah's name forever and ever. Has He not
Himself said, *"My praise shall be of thee in the great
congregation"* (Psalm 22:25)?

What do these dark sayings, so hard to understand, really mean?

> *Then cometh the end, when he shall have deliv-
> ered up the kingdom to God, even the Father....
> And when all things shall be subdued unto him,
> then shall the Son also himself be subject unto
> him that put all things under him, that God may
> be all in all.* (1 Corinthians 15:24, 28)

Whatever those words may mean, they seem to teach
us that the intermediate crown and government are
temporary, that they are intended to last only until
all rule and all authority and power are put down by
Jesus and until the rule of God is universally ac-
knowledged. Jesus cannot renounce His Godhead,
but His temporary sovereignty will be yielded up to
Him from whom it came. That last solemn act, in
which Christ hands back to His Father the
all-subduing scepter, will be a praising of God to
such a wonderful extent that it is beyond human
conception. We wait and watch for it, and we will
behold it in the appointed time.

Beloved friends, we also have an example in this second part of our text: let us endeavor to praise our God in a direct manner. We ought to spend at least a little time every day in adoring contemplation. Our private devotions are scarcely complete if they consist only of prayer. They need the element of praise, too. If possible, during each day, sing a hymn or a chorus. Perhaps you are not in a position to sing it aloud—very loud, at any rate—but I would hum it over, if I were you. Many of you laborers find time enough to sing a silly song; why can you not find time for the praise of God? Every day let us praise Him, when the eyelids of the morning first are opened, and when the curtains of the night are drawn. And, yes, if we awaken at the midnight hour, let our hearts put fire to the sacred incense and present it unto the Lord who lives forever and ever.

"In the midst of the congregation" also, whenever we come up to God's house, let us take care that our praise is not merely lip service, but that of the heart. Let us all sing, and so sing that God Himself hears. We need more than the sweet sounds that die upon mortal ears. We want the deep melodies that spring from the heart and that enter into the ears of the immortal God. Imitate Jesus, then, in this two-fold praise, the declaring of God and the giving of direct praise to Him.

OUR LORD'S EXHORTATION TO PRAISE

Follow me earnestly, my friends, and then follow me practically also. In the second verse of our text, our Lord is exhorting us to praise God Almighty: *"Ye that fear the LORD, praise him; all ye the seed of Jacob, glorify him; and fear him, all ye the seed of Israel."*

This appeal is directed to those who fear God, who have respect for Him, who tremble lest they offend Him, who carry with them the consciousness of His presence into their daily lives, who act toward Him as obedient children toward a father. The exhortation is further addressed to *"the seed of Jacob"*: to those in covenant with God; to those who have despised the pottage and chosen the birthright; to those who, if they have had to sleep with stones for their pillows, have nevertheless seen heaven opened and enjoyed a revelation of God; to those who know what prevailing in prayer means; to those who, in all their trouble, have yet found that all these things are not against them, but work together for their everlasting good; to those who know that Jesus is yet alive and that they will see Him when they die. It is, moreover, directed to *"the seed of Israel"*: to those who once were in Egypt and in spiritual bondage; to those who have been brought out of slavery, who are being guided through the wilderness, fed with heaven's manna, and made to drink of the living Rock; to those who worship the one God and Him only, who put away their idols, and who desire to be found obedient to the Master's will.

Vocal Praise

Now, to them it is said, first of all, *"Praise him."* Praise the Lord vocally. I wish that in every congregation every child of God would take pains to praise God with his mouth as well as with his heart. I have noticed something in my own congregation, which I have jotted down in the pages of my memory, and which I believe to be generally true: you always sing best when you are most spiritually focused. There are definitely times of worship when your singing is very much better than it is at other times. You keep better time and better tune, not because the tune is any easier, but because you desire to worship God with more solemnity than usual. Thus, there is no slovenly singing such as that which sometimes pains the ear and heart. Why, some of you care so little to give the Lord your best music that you fall half a beat behind the rest, others of you are singing quite off-key, and a few make no sound of any kind! I hate to enter a place of worship where half a dozen sing to the praise and glory of themselves, while the rest stand and listen.

I like that good old plan of everybody singing, singing his best, singing carefully and heartily. If you cannot sing artistically, never mind, you will be right enough if you sing from the heart and pay attention to it. Just do not drawl out like a musical machine that has been set agoing and therefore runs on mechanically. With a little care the heart brings the art, and the heart desiring to praise will train the voice to the time and tune by and by.

I would like our worship services to be the best. I personally do not care for the fineries of music and the excellencies of chants and anthems. As for instrumental music, I fear that it often destroys the singing of the congregation and detracts from the spirituality and simplicity of worship. If I could crowd a house twenty times as big as my church with the fine music that some churches delight in, God forbid I should touch it. Rather, let us have the best and most orderly harmony we can make—let the saints come with their hearts in the best of moods and their voices in the best tune, and let them take care that there be no slovenliness or discord in the public worship of the Most High.

Mental Praise

Take care to mentally praise God also. The grandest praise that floats up to the throne is that which arises from silent contemplation and reverent thought. Sit down and think of the greatness of God, His love, His power, His faithfulness, His sovereignty, and as your mind bows prostrate before His majesty, you will have praised Him, though not a sound will have come from you.

Active Praise

Praise God also by your actions. Your sacrifice to Him of your property, your offering to Him week by week of your substance, your giving of your time and energy to *"the least of these* [His] *brethren"* (Matthew 25:40) is true praise, and far less likely to be hypocritical than mere words of thanksgiving. *"Ye that fear the Lord, praise him."*

Glorifying Praise

Our text adds, *"All ye the seed of Jacob, glorify him."* This is another form of the same thing. Glorify God; let others know of His glory. Let them know of it from what you say, but especially let them know of it from what you are and how you act. Glorify God in your business, in your recreations, in your shops, and in your households. *"Whether therefore ye eat, or drink, or whatsoever ye do, do all to the glory of God"* (1 Corinthians 10:31). In the commonest actions of life, wear the vestments of your sacred calling, and act as a royal priesthood, serving the Most High.

Glorify your Creator and Redeemer. Glorify Him by endeavoring to spread abroad the Gospel that glorifies Him. Magnify Christ by explaining to men how, by believing, they will find peace in Him. Glorify God by boldly relying on His word for yourself, in the teeth of afflicting providence, and over the head of all suspicions and mistrust. Nothing can glorify God more than an Abrahamic faith that *"stagger*[s] *not at the promise of God through unbelief"* (Romans 4:20). O you wrestling seed of Jacob, see to it that you do not falter in the matter of glorifying your God.

Awesome, Sinless Praise

The last thing mentioned in our text is to *"fear him,"* as if this were one of the highest methods of praise. Walk in His sight; constantly keep the Lord before you; let Him be at your right hand. Sin not, for in sinning you dishonor Him. Suffer rather than sin. Choose the burning fiery furnace rather than bow down before the golden image. Be willing to be despised yourself rather than that God should be despised. Be content to bear the cross rather than allow Jesus to be crucified afresh (Hebrews 6:6). Be put to shame rather than allow Jesus to suffer any more shame. Thus, you will truly praise and magnify the name of the Most High.

THE PRACTICE OF PRAISE

I must close this chapter with a few remarks that are meant to assist you in carrying out the practice of this teaching. Beloved brothers and sisters, this morning I felt, before I began to write, very much in the spirit of adoring gratitude. I cannot communicate that to you, but the Spirit of God can. The thoughts that helped me to praise God were something like these (let me give them to you as applied to yourselves): glorify and praise God, for He has saved you, saved you from hell, saved you for heaven. Oh, how much is encompassed by the fact that you are saved! Think of the election that ordained you to salvation, the covenant that assured salvation to you. Think of the incarnation by which God came to you. Consider the precious blood by which you now have been *"made nigh"* (Ephesians 2:13) to God.

Do not hurry over those thoughts, even though I must shorten my words. Linger at each one of these sacred fountains and drink. When you have seen what salvation involved in the past, think of what it means in the future. You will be preserved to the end. You will be educated in the school of grace. You will be admitted into the home of the blessed in the land of the hereafter. You will have a resurrection most glorious and an immortality most illustrious. When days and years will have passed, a crown will adorn your brow, and a harp of joy will fill your hand. All of this is yours, believer. Will you not praise Him?

Make any one of these blessings stand out in your mind, as personally real to you, and I think you will say, "Should I refuse to sing, surely the very stones would cry out" (Luke 19:40).

Your God has done more than this for you. You are not barely saved, like a drowning man just dragged to the bank; you have had more given to you than you ever lost. You have gained by Adam's fall. You might almost say, as one of the fathers did, "O *felix culpa,* O happy fault, that put me into the position to be so richly endowed as now I am!" Had you stood in Adam, you would never have been able to call Jesus "Brother," for there would have been no need for Him to become incarnate. You would never have been washed in His precious blood, for then it had no need to be shed.

Jesus has restored to you what He did not take away in the first place. He has not merely lifted you from the trash heap to set you among men, but to set you among princes, even the princes of His people, and to make you inherit the throne of glory (1 Samuel 2:8). Think of the bright roll of promises, of the rich treasure of covenant provision, of all that you have already had and all that Christ has guaranteed to you of honor and glory and immortality. Will you not praise the Lord *"in the midst of the congregation"*?

Beloved brothers and sisters, some of us have special cause for praising God in the fact that we have recently seen many saved, and among them those dear to us. Mothers, can you hear this fact without joy? Your children are saved! Brothers, your sisters are saved! Fathers, your sons and daughters are saved! How many has God brought in lately that you have been privileged to know about? You Sunday school teachers who have been the instruments of this, you conductors of classes who have been honored by God to be spiritual parents, you elders and deacons and intercessors who have prayed so willingly with these converts—all of you who now share the joy in these conversions, will you not bless God? *"Not unto us, O LORD, not unto us, but unto thy name* [we] *give glory, for thy mercy, and for thy truth's sake"* (Psalm 115:1). Oh, we cannot be silent! Not one tongue must be silent; we will all magnify and bless the Most High.

Beloved friends, if these facts do not suffice to make us praise Him, I would say, think of the glorious God! Think of Father, Son, and Spirit, and what the triune Jehovah is in His own person and attributes. If you do not praise Him then, how far must you have backslidden!

Remember the host who now adore Him. When we bless Him, we do not stand alone: angels and archangels are at our right hand; cherubim and seraphim are in the same choir. The notes of redeemed men do not sound alone; they are united to, and swollen by, the unceasing flood of praise that flows from the hierarchy of angels.

Think, beloved, of how you will praise Him soon and how, before much time has passed, many of us will be with the glorious throng! Recently you have probably seen some of your friends and relatives having been translated to the skies: more links to heaven, fewer bonds to earth. They have gone before you, and to this you have almost said, "Would God it were me instead of them!" They have now seen what eye has not seen, and heard what ear has never heard, and their spirits have drunk in what they could not otherwise have conceived.

The Fullness of Joy

We will soon join that heavenly choir! Meanwhile, let each one of us sing:

> I would begin the music here,
>   And so my soul should rise:
> Oh, for some heavenly notes to bear
>   My passions to the skies!
>
> There ye that love my Savior sit,
>   There I would fain have place
> Among your thrones, or at your feet,
>   So I might see His face.

Chapter Three

Marvelous Things

O sing unto the LORD a new song; for he hath done marvellous things: his right hand, and his holy arm, hath gotten him the victory. The LORD hath made known his salvation: his righteousness hath he openly showed in the sight of the heathen.
—Psalm 98:1–2

The invitations of the Gospel are invitations to happiness. In delivering God's message, we do not ask men to come to a funeral, but to a wedding feast. If our errand were one of sorrow, we might not marvel when people refuse to listen to us. But, it is one of gladness, not sadness. In fact, you might condense the gospel message into this joyous invitation: "O come, and learn how to *"sing unto the LORD a new song"*! Come, and find peace, rest, joy, and all else that your soul can desire. Come, and *'eat ye that which is good, and let your soul delight itself in fatness'"* (Isaiah 55:2). When the coming of Christ to the earth was first announced, it was not with sad, sonorous sounds of evil spirits, driven from the nethermost hell, but with the choral symphonies of holy angels who joyfully sang, *"Glory to God in the highest, and on earth peace, good will toward men"* (Luke 2:14).

THE GOSPEL, OUR SOURCE OF JOY

As long as the Gospel is preached in this world, its main message will be one of joy. The Gospel is a source of joy to those who proclaim it, for unto us, *"who* [are] *less than the least of all saints, is this grace given, that* [we] *should preach among the Gentiles the unsearchable riches of Christ"* (Ephesians 3:8). The Gospel is also a source of joy to all who really hear it and accept it, for its very name means "glad tidings of good things."

I feel that if I am not able to witness as I would like, still I am overjoyed in being permitted to proclaim the Gospel at all. If the style and manner of my words are not such as I desire them to be or such as you endorse, yet it matters little, for the simplest telling of the Gospel is a most delightful thing in itself. If our hearts are in a right condition, we would not only be glad to hear of Jesus over and over again, but the story of the love of God Incarnate, and of the redemption brought about by Immanuel, would be the sweetest music that our ears ever heard.

In the hope that our hearts may thus rejoice, I am going to address many points about two general areas: the marvelous things God has done in the person of His Son, and some marvelous things in reference to ourselves, which are almost as marvelous as those that God has done in Christ.

I call your attention to the marvelous tidings mentioned in our text. If you read it carefully, you will notice that, first, there are some marvelous things that are amazing in themselves: *"He hath done marvellous things."* Secondly, there are some that are wonderful in the way in which they were done: *"His right hand, and his holy arm, hath gotten him the victory."* Then, there are some that are marvelous as to the way in which they were made known: *"The LORD hath made known his salvation: his righteousness hath he openly showed in the sight of the heathen."*

SIMPLY MARVELOUS THINGS

Let us consider the things that are wonderful in themselves: *"He hath done marvellous things: his right hand, and his holy arm, hath gotten him the victory."* You know the story. We were enslaved by sin; we were in such bondage that we were liable to be forever in chains. However, our great Champion undertook our cause, entered the lists, and pledged to fight for us until the end; and He has done it. It would have been a cause of great joy if I could have said to you, "The Lord Jesus Christ has undertaken to fight our battles for us," but I have something much better than that to say. He has fought the fight, and *"his holy arm, hath gotten him the victory."*

It must have required more faith to believe in the Christ who was to come than to believe in the Christ who has come. It must have required no little faith to believe in Christ as victorious while He was in the midst of the struggle; for instance, when His bloody sweat was falling amid the olive trees, or when He was hanging upon the cross and moaning out that awful cry: *"My God, my God, why hast thou forsaken me?"* (Matthew 27:46). But the great crisis is past. No longer does the issue of the conflict tremble in the balance: Christ has forever accomplished His warfare, and our foes are all beneath His feet.

> Love's redeeming work is done;
> Fought the light, the battle won.

Christ Overcame Sin

What foes has Christ overcome? Our main foe, our sin, both as to the guilt of it and as to the power of it. As to the guilt of it, there was the law, which we have broken and which must be satisfied. Christ has kept the positive precepts of that law in His own perfect life, and He has vindicated the honor of that law by His sacrificial death on the cross. Therefore, the law being satisfied, the strength of sin is gone.

Now, believers, the sins that you saw in the time of your conviction you will never see again! As Moses triumphantly sang of the enemies of the chosen people, *"the depths have covered them: they sank into the bottom as a stone"* (Exodus 15:5), so can you say of your sins, "There is not one of them left; they have been cast *'into the depths of the sea'"* (Micah 7:19).

Even in God's great Book of Remembrance there is no record of sin against any believer in the Lord Jesus Christ. *"By him all that believe are justified from all things"* (Acts 13:39). Try to realize this, brothers and sisters in Christ. Let the great army of your sins pass before you in review, each one like a son of Anak, a giant (Numbers 13:33) armed to the hilt for your destruction. They have gone down into the depths, and the red sea of Christ's blood has drowned them. Thus, He has gained a complete victory over all the guilt of sin.

As for the power of sin within us, we often groan concerning it, but let us groan no longer. Or, if we do, let us also *"sing unto the LORD a new song."*

The experience of a Christian is summed up in Paul's utterance, *"O wretched man that I am! who shall deliver me from the body of this death? I thank God through Jesus Christ our Lord"* (Romans 7:24–25). If you take the whole quotation, I believe you have a summary of a spiritual man's life: a daily groaning and a daily boasting, a daily humbling and a daily rejoicing, a daily consciousness of sin and a daily consciousness of the power of the Lord Jesus Christ to conquer it.

We do believe, beloved, that our sin has received its deathblow. It still lingers within us, for its death is by crucifixion, and crucifixion is a lingering death. Its heart is not altogether fastened to the cross, but its hands are, so that we cannot sin as we once did. Its feet, too, are fastened, so that we cannot run in the way of transgressors as we once did. And one of these days, the spear will pierce its heart, and it will utterly die. Then, with the faultless ones before the throne of God, we will be unattended by depravity or corruption any longer. Therefore, let us *"sing unto the LORD a new song,"* because *"his right hand, and his holy arm, hath gotten him the victory"* over sin within us.

> His be the victor's name,
>   Who fought our fight alone;
> Triumphant saints no honor claim;
>   His conquest was His own.

The Fullness of Joy

Christ Conquered Death

In connection with sin came death, for death is the daughter of sin and follows closely upon sin. Jesus has conquered death. It is not possible for believers to die eternally, for Jesus said, *"Because I live, ye shall live also"* (John 14:19). Even the character of the natural death is changed for believers. It is not now a penal infliction, but a necessary way of elevating our nature from the bondage of corruption into the glorious liberty of the children of God, for *"flesh and blood cannot inherit the kingdom of God"* (1 Corinthians 15:50). Even those who will be living at the coming of the Lord must be bodily changed in order that they may be fit to enter glory. Death, therefore, to believers, is but a putting off of our weekday garments so that we may put on our Sunday best, the laying aside of the travel-stained clothes of earth so that we may put on the pure garments of joy forever.

Thus, we do not fear death now, for Christ has conquered it. He has torn away the iron bars of the grave; He has left His own shroud and napkin in the sepulcher so that there might be suitable furniture in what was once a grim, cold, empty tomb; and He has gone up into His glory and left heaven's gate wide open to all believers. Unless He first comes again, we, too, will descend into the grave where He went; but we will also come up again as He did, and we will rise, complete in the perfection of our redeemed humanity. Then, when we awake in the likeness of our Master, we will be satisfied. So let us *"sing unto the LORD a new song; for he hath done marvellous things."*

Marvelous Things

Hosannah to the Prince of light,
    Who clothed Himself in clay,
Entered the iron gates of death,
    And tore the bars away!

Death is no more the king of dread
    Since our Immanuel rose.
He took the tyrant's sting away,
    And spoiled our hellish foes.

See how the Conqueror mounts aloft,
    And to His Father flies,
With scars of honor in His flesh
    And triumph in His eyes.

Christ Defeated Satan

Just as Christ has conquered sin and death, so has He conquered the Devil and all his hosts of fallen spirits. This monster of iniquity, this monster of craft and malice, has striven to hold us in perpetual bondage. However, Christ met him in the wilderness and vanquished him there. Also, I believe, Christ met him in personal conflict in the Garden of Gethsemane, where He vanquished him once and for all. And now, He has *"led captivity captive"* (Ephesians 4:8). Inferior spirits were driven away by Christ when He was here upon earth, and they fled at the bidding of the King. And now, although Satan still worries and vexes the saints of God, *"the God of peace shall bruise Satan under* [our] *feet shortly"* (Romans 16:20).

Therefore, dearly beloved in Christ, this is the joyous news we have to bring to sinners: sin and death and the Devil have all been vanquished by the great Captain of our salvation. For this reason, let us so rejoice that we *"sing unto the LORD a new song."*

In hell, He laid hell low;
  Made sin, He sin o'erthrew:
Bowed to the grave, destroyed it so,
  And death, by dying, slew.

Sin, Satan, death appear
  To harass and appall;
Yet since the gracious Lord is near,
  Backward they go, and fall.

THE MARVELOUS WAYS OF THE LORD

According to our text, what the Lord did is not only marvelous in itself, but the way in which He did it was also amazing. Observe that He did it alone: *"His* [own] *right hand, and His holy arm, hath gotten him the victory."* No one was associated with the Lord Jesus Christ in the conquest that He achieved over sin and death and the Devil, and nothing is more abhorrent to a believing soul than the idea of giving any bit of glory to anyone but the Lord Jesus Christ. He trod *"the winepress alone"* (Isaiah 63:3), so let Him alone wear the crown.

Sinner, you do not have to look for any secondary savior, for Christ is the only Savior you need: He has done it all. You do not need to pay reverence to any saints or martyrs or priests. Christ has done it all, so seek Him for all you want, and honor Him as the one true source of all you need. Christ alone has accomplished the salvation of His people; no other hand has been raised to help Him in the fight. Look then to Jesus alone for salvation. Trust in Him with your whole heart. Throw your weight entirely upon Him, my poor lost soul, if you have not yet done so, and you will find rest and salvation in Him.

Marvelous Things

The Wisdom of His Ways

Another wonder is that He did it all so wisely: *"His right hand...hath gotten him the victory."* You know that today the word *dexterous* is used to signify a thing that is skillfully done. However, its original Latin root word means something that is done with the right hand and is thus done with adeptness and mastery. Thus, when Christ fought our battle with His right hand, He did it with ease, with strength, and with infinite wisdom.

The design of salvation is the very perfection of wisdom, because all the attributes of God are equally glorified in it. There is as much justice as there is mercy in a sinner's salvation by the atoning sacrifice of Christ. Salvation reveals God's complete mercy as well as His total justice: God fulfilled His threatenings against sin by smiting Christ and gave the love of His heart full expression in saving even the chief of sinners through the death of His dear Son.

The more I consider the doctrine of substitution, the more my soul is enamored with the matchless wisdom of God that devised this system of salvation. As for a hazy atonement that atones for everybody in general and for nobody in particular—an atonement made equally for Judas and for John—I care nothing for it. But a literal, substitutionary sacrifice—Christ vicariously bearing the wrath of God on my behalf— this calms my conscience with regard to the righteous demands of the law of God and satisfies the instincts of my nature, which declare that, since God is just, He must exact the penalty of my guilt.

Dear believers, in suffering, bleeding, and dying, Jesus Christ has gotten us the victory. The hand that was pierced by the nails has conquered sin; the hand that was fastened to the wood has fastened up the accusation that was written against us; the hand that bled has brought salvation to us, so that we are Christ's forever. Infinite wisdom shone through in our Lord's conquest of sin and death and the Devil.

The Holiness of His Ways

But, holiness was also involved: *"His holy arm, hath gotten him the victory."* The psalmist seemed, as he progressed in his worship, to fall more and more in love with the matchless holiness of God. The holiness of the victory of Christ is a wonderful thing to glorify, for there is never a sinner so saved as to make God's eyes seem to wink at sin. Since the creation of this world, there was never an act of mercy performed by God that was not in perfect harmony with the severest justice. God, although He has loved and saved unholy men, has never stained His holy hands in the act of saving them. He remains the *"holy, holy, holy, Lord God Almighty"* (Revelation 4:8), although He is still very full of pity and compassion as He passes by transgression, iniquity, and sin, and presses prodigal children to His heart.

The Atonement through the shed blood of Jesus Christ is the answer to these great questions: How can God be just and yet the Justifier of those who believe? How can He be perfectly holy and yet, at the same time, receive into His love and adopt into His family those who are unrighteous and unholy? O Calvary, you have solved the problem. In the bleeding wounds of our Savior, *"righteousness and peace have kissed each other"* (Psalm 85:10).

May God grant you, unconverted sinner, the grace to understand how He can save you, yet be perfectly holy; how He can forgive your sins, yet be perfectly just! I know this is the difficulty that troubles you: How can you be received while God is what He is, *"the Judge of all"* (Hebrews 12:23)? He can receive you because the Lord Jesus Christ took the sins of His people and bore them *"in his own body on the tree"* (1 Peter 2:24). Thus, being the appointed Head of all believers, Christ has vindicated in His own person the inflexible justice of God. Here is the Man who has kept the whole law of God—not Adam, for he failed to keep it. However, the Second Adam, the Lord from heaven, and all whom He represented are now *"accepted in the beloved"* (Ephesians 1:6); they are made acceptable to God because of what Jesus Christ has done. So let us magnify *"his holy arm,* [which] *hath gotten him the victory."*

THE LORD'S MARVELOUS GRACE

I now want to look at the marvelous grace that has revealed all this to us. It is a very familiar thing today for us to hear the Gospel, but will you just carry your minds back some two or three thousand years to the period when Psalm 98 was written? What was then known concerning salvation was known almost exclusively by the Jews. Here and there, a proselyte was led into the bonds of the covenant; but for the most part, the whole world lay in heathen darkness. Where there was the seal of circumcision, there were the oracles of God; but the Gentile sinners knew nothing whatever concerning the truth. And it might have been that way until this day if the Lord had not *"made known his salvation:* [and] *his righteousness...in the sight of the heathen."* Our present privileges are greater than the privileges of the ancient Israelites, of those whom, I am afraid, we sometimes despise—or at least forget—of those whom we have for a moment supplanted. They were the favored people of God. Through their unbelief, they have been set aside for a while, but Israel is yet to be restored to even greater blessings than it formerly experienced.

> The hymn shall yet in Zion swell
> That sounds Messiah's praise,
> And Thy loved name, Immanuel!
> As once in ancient days.
>
> For Israel yet shall own her King,
> For her salvation waits.
> And hill and dale shall sweetly sing
> With praise in all her gates!

Do we value as we ought the privilege we now have of hearing in our own language the wonderful works of God? My dear unconverted reader, how grateful you ought to be that you ware not born in Rome or Babylon or the far-off Indies, in those days when there was no Christian missionary to seek you out and care for your soul, but when all of the light that shone was shed upon that little land of Israel! Jesus Christ has *"broken down the middle wall of partition"* (Ephesians 2:14). Now it makes no difference whether we are *"Barbarian, Scythian, bond* [or] *free"* (Colossians 3:11). The Gospel is to be preached to every creature in all the world (Mark 16:15). Moreover, *"he that believeth and is baptized shall be saved"* (v. 16), no matter what the person's previous character may have been or to what race he may have belonged.

The Holy Spirit's Wonderful Revelation

Yet, let us never forget that, in order to accomplish this great work of salvation, it was necessary that the blessed Son of God descend to this world. It was also necessary that the Spirit of God be given to rest upon the church, to be the inspiration by which the Gospel should be preached among the heathen. Again let me ask a question: Do we sufficiently reverence the Holy Spirit and love Him as we should for all that He has done?

The incarnation of the Son of God is no greater mystery than the indwelling of the Spirit of God in the hearts of men. It is truly marvelous that the Holy Spirit, who is equally God with the Father and the Son, should come and reside in these bodies of ours and make them His temple. Yet, remember that, if it had not been so, there would have been no effective preaching of the Gospel. Further, unless the Holy Spirit blesses the Word right now, there will be no open showing of Christ's righteousness to you and no making known of His salvation to your heart. All the victories of Christ, for which I urge your grateful songs, would be unknown to you if the Holy Spirit did not touch men's lips so that they might tell what the Lord has done and publish abroad His glorious victories.

Remember, too, that, in connection with the work of the Holy Spirit, there has had to be an unbroken chain of divine providence to bring the Gospel to you and to your land. Look back through the past ages, and see what wonderful revolutions of the wheels full of eyes (Ezekiel 10:12) there have been. Empires have risen and have fallen, but their rise and fall have had a close connection with the preaching of the Gospel. There have been terrific persecutions of the saints of God. Satan has seemed to summon all the forces of hell to attack the church of Christ, yet he could not destroy its life. There came the dark night of the dogmatic popes, dense as the nights of Egypt's darkness; but old Rome could not put out the light of the Gospel.

Since then, in what marvelous ways has God led His chosen people! He has raised up His servants, one after another, so that the testimony concerning the victories achieved by Christ might be continued among us and might be spread throughout all the nations of the earth. Thus, it has come to pass that you can now have an open Bible in your hands and that I can freely explain the teaching of that Bible to you. How wonderfully has the history of our own country been working toward this happy result! Glorify God and bless His holy name that we live in such golden days as these, when *"the LORD hath made known his salvation,"* and *"his righteousness hath he openly showed in the sight of the heathen."*

A Greater Revelation of Grace

Further, let us more sweetly praise the Lord that we not only live where the Gospel is made known, but that God has made it known to some of us in a still deeper sense. Some of us now understand, as we did not at one time, the righteousness of God—His way of making man righteous through Jesus Christ.

We understood it in theory long before God made it savingly known in our souls. This is another work of the Holy Spirit for which we have good reason to *"sing unto the LORD a new song."*

Sinner, God has sent the Gospel to you to tell you that His Son, Jesus Christ, has conquered sin and death and the Devil, and that, if you believe in Jesus, you will be a partaker in His victory. There is nothing for you to do but to believe in Him. Even the power to understand His truth is God's gift to you; even the faith that receives His truth He works in you according to His Spirit. You are to be nothing so that God may be everything. It is for you to fall at His feet, with confusion of face and contrition of heart. Then, when He bids you do so, you need to rise up and say, "I will sing a new song unto the Lord. *'O LORD, I will praise thee: though thou wast angry with me, thine anger is turned away, and thou comfortedst me'* (Isaiah 12:1) through Him who won the victory on my behalf."

AMAZING THINGS IN REFERENCE TO MANKIND

The second part of this subject, which I will touch on very briefly, is this: there are some astonishing things in reference to ourselves.

Man's Astounding Indifference

The first of these marvelous things is that after all that Christ has done, and after the mercy of God has made His salvation known, so many people are utterly careless and indifferent concerning it. Tens of thousands will not even cross the threshold of a church to go and hear about it. Bibles are in many of their houses, yet they do not take the time to read them. If they are going on a railway journey, they consult their train schedule, but they do not search God's own Guidebook to find the way to heaven or to learn where and when they must start if they intend to reach that place of eternal happiness and bliss. We can still ask, *"Who hath believed our report? and to whom is the arm of the LORD revealed?"* (Isaiah 53:1).

To me, the most astonishing sight is an unconverted man outside of hell. It is a marvel of marvels that the Son of God Himself left all the glories of heaven and came to earth to bleed and die, in man's shape for man's sake, and yet that there could be anyone in the shape of a man who would not care even to hear the story of His wondrous sacrifice. It is a wonder that anyone, upon hearing the story, could disregard it as if it were of no interest to him. Yet, see how men rush to buy a newspaper when there is some little bit of news! With what eagerness do some young people—and some old people, too, who ought to know better—await the next episode of a foolish serial story of a lovesick maid! How freely their tears flow over imaginary griefs! However, the Lord Jesus Christ, bleeding to death in unconditional love for His enemies, does not move them to tears, and their hearts remain untouched by the story of His sufferings as if they were made of marble.

The Astonishing Depravity of Mankind

The depravity of mankind is a miracle of sin; it is as great a miracle, from one point of view, as the grace of God is from another. Jesus Christ neglected! Eternal love slighted! Infinite mercy disregarded! I have to confess, with great shame, that even the preacher of the Gospel is not always affected by it as he ought to be; not only must I confess this, but so must others, I fear, who preach the Word of God. Why, it ought to make us dance for joy to tell our congregations that there is mercy in the heart of God, that there is pardon for sinners, that there is life for the dead, that the great heart of God yearns over sinners. Our hearts ought to be ready to break when we find that men disregard all this good news and are not affected by it. It is an astounding calamity that men should have fallen so terribly that infinite love is imperceptible by them. May God grant that His grace show to you, unconverted sinners, in what a horrible state your hearts must be, because, after all that Christ has done, you still give Him no token of gratitude, no song of praise for the wonders He has performed.

The Marvel That Any Are Saved

Looking from this point of view, we see another marvelous thing: that some of us have been so enabled to recognize the work of Christ that we are saved by it. To confess the truth, there are some of us who were very unlikely candidates for salvation. Probably, each saved individual reading this has thought himself to be the most unlikely person ever to be saved. I know that I thought so concerning myself.

I recall the story of a Scotsman who went to see Mr. Rowland Hill. For a long while he sat, staring at

Rowland in the face, until the good old minister asked him, "What are you looking at?" The Scotsman replied, "I have been studying the lines of your face." "What do you make of them?" asked Rowland. The answer was, "I was thinking what a great vagabond you would have been if the grace of God had not met with you." "That thought has often struck me," replied Rowland.

A similar thought has often struck most of us. If we had not been converted, would we have led others into sin? Would we have invented fresh pleasures of vice and folly? Who would have stopped us? We had daring enough for anything, enough even to have defied the very Devil himself, if we had thought that some new vice could have been invented or some fresh pleasure of sin could have been discovered. But now that God has made us yield, has subdued us by His sovereign grace, has brought us to His feet, and has put on us the chains that now we gladly welcome, and that we long to wear forever, *"O* [let us] *sing unto the LORD a new song; for he hath done marvellous things* [for us]: *his right hand, and his holy arm, hath gotten him the victory."*

Dear child of God, if there has been special grace in your case, as I know you feel that there has been, you ought to give special honor to Christ. Everyone who is saved ought to live a very special life—an extraordinary life. If you were an extraordinary sinner, or have been an extraordinary debtor to divine love in some way or other, may there be some extraordinary devotion, some extraordinary consecration, some extraordinary faith, some extraordinary liberality, some extraordinary lovingkindness, or some other extraordinary thing about you in which the traces of that marvelous right hand of God and His holy arm will be plainly manifested!

The Marvelous Joy of the Believer

The last thing I want to address is this: there is something marvelous in the joy that we, who have believed in the victory secured by Christ, have received. Probably all of you have sung that song with the refrain, "I am so glad that Jesus loves me." That refrain is very monotonous, yet I think I would like to sing it all night and would not want to stop, even when the morning sun arose.

> I am so glad that Jesus loves me;
> I am so glad that Jesus loves me;
> I am so glad that Jesus loves me,
> I'm singing, glory, hallelujah,
> Jesus loves me.

"I am so glad that Jesus loves me." You may turn it over and over and over and over, as long as you like, but you will never find anything that makes you so glad as the realization that Jesus loves you. You will never find that the sweetness of the thought, "Jesus loves me," will ever be exhausted.

Sinner, if you only knew the blessedness of the life of Christ, you would be overjoyed to run away from your own life and run to share ours in Him! We have peace like a river. We can leave all our cares and our burdens with our God. We are just where we love most to be—in the bosom of our heavenly Father—and the Spirit of adoption makes us feel perfectly at home with Him. We can all say, *"Return unto thy rest, O my soul; for the LORD hath dealt bountifully with thee"* (Psalm 116:7). We are in perfect safety, for who can destroy those whom Christ protects? We have a perfect peace even with our own conscience. We have also a blessed prospect for the future: we will be borne along upon the wings of divine providence until we reach the golden shores of our eternal home. We have a heaven below, and we are looking for a still better heaven above.

> All that remains for me
> Is but to love and sing,
> And wait until the angels come
> To bear me to the King.

This is the lower, earthly part of the choir. Some of the singers are up in the galleries, and we are learning here the notes that we will sing above. Come, beloved, let us make these sinners yearn to share our joys. If any of you saints have been moaning and groaning of late, get into a proper attitude of mind. Begin to tune up and to praise the Lord with all your might until the ungodly shall say, "After all, there is something sweeter and brighter and better in the lives of these Christians than we have ever known in ours."

However, whether you will rejoice or not, *"my soul doth magnify the Lord, and my spirit hath rejoiced in God my Saviour"* (Luke 1:46–47); and I will continue, by His help, until death suspends these mortal songs or blends them into the immortal melodies before the throne.

Chapter Four

Christ's Joy and Ours

These things have I spoken unto you, that my joy might remain in you, and that your joy might be full.
—John 15:11

A common saying has crept in among our proverbs, which is being repeated as if it were altogether true: "Man was made to mourn." There is an element of truth in that sentence, but there is also a falsehood in it. Man was not originally made to mourn; he was made to rejoice. The Garden of Eden was his place of happy abode, and as long as he continued in obedience to God, nothing grew in that Garden that could cause him sorrow. For his delight, the flowers breathed out their perfume. For his pleasure, the landscapes were full of beauty, and the rivers rippled over golden sands. God made human beings, as He made His other creatures, to be happy. They are capable of happiness. They are in their right element when they are happy.

The Fullness of Joy

Now that Jesus Christ has come to restore the ruins of the Fall, He has come to bring back to us the old joy—only it will be even sweeter and deeper than it could have been if we had never lost it. A Christian has never fully realized what Christ came to make him until he has grasped the joy of the Lord. Christ wants His people to be happy. When they are perfect, as He will make them in due time, they will also be perfectly happy. As heaven is the place of pure holiness, so is it the place of sheer happiness. In proportion to our increasing readiness for heaven, we will have some of the joy that belongs to heaven.

OUR FULL JOY IS CHRIST'S WILL

My first observation about our text is this: all that Jesus spoke in the past and all that He speaks today through His Word is meant to produce joy in His people: *"These things have I spoken unto you, that my joy might remain in you, and that your joy may be full."* It is our Savior's will that, even now, we should dwell and abide in the fullness of His joy.

Words of Instruction

If you will read through the fifteenth chapter of John, from which our text is taken, and also the chapter that precedes it, you will see the nature of the words that Jesus Christ speaks to His people. Sometimes they are words of instruction. He talks to us in order that we may know the truth and the meaning of the truth. However, His objective is that, in knowing the truth, we may have joy in it.

I will not say that the more a Christian knows, the more joy he has, but I can truly say that ignorance often hides from us many wells of delight of which we might otherwise drink. Generally, all other things being equal, the best instructed Christian will be the happiest person. He will know the truth, and the truth will make him free (John 8:32). The truth will kill a thousand fears that ignorance would have fostered within him.

The knowledge of the love of God, the knowledge of the full Atonement made on Calvary, the knowledge of the eternal covenant, the knowledge of the immutable faithfulness of Jehovah—indeed, all knowledge that reveals God in His relationship to His people—will tend to create comfort in the hearts of His saints. Therefore, do not be careless about scriptural doctrine. Study the Word, and seek to understand the mind of the Spirit as revealed in it, for this blessed Book was written for your learning, that *"through patience and comfort of the scriptures* [you] *might have hope"* (Romans 15:4). If you are diligent students of the Word, you will find that you have good reason to rejoice in the Lord in all circumstances.

Words of Warning

Sometimes our Lord speaks words of warning to us, as He did while He was on earth. In the fifteenth chapter of John, we discover that He told His disciples that they were branches of a vine, and that branches bearing no fruit had to be cut off and cast into the fire. At first, it seems to us that nothing is consoling in such words as those. They sound sharply in our ears, startling us, making each of us fearfully ask himself, "Am I bearing fruit?" Well, beloved, such soul-searching as that is exceptionally beneficial, because it tends to deepen in us true joy. Christ would not have us rejoice with the false joy of presumption, so He takes the sharp knife and cuts that mistaken joy away. Joy on a false basis would prevent us from having true joy. Therefore, the Master gives us the sharp, cutting word so that we will be sound in our faith, so that we will be sound in the life of God, and so that the joy we receive will be worth having—not the mere foam of a wave that is driven with the wind and tossed, but the solid foundation of the Rock of Ages.

Our Lord also tells us that even branches that are bearing fruit have to be pruned in order for them to bring forth more fruit (John 15:2). "What an unpleasant truth!" somebody might say. "It gives me no joy to know that I have to endure the knife of correction and affliction." Yes, dear one, but remember this:

> *And not only so, but we glory in tribulations also: knowing that tribulation worketh patience; and patience, experience; and experience, hope: and hope maketh not ashamed; because the love of God is shed abroad in our hearts by the Holy Ghost which is given unto us.* (Romans 5:3–5)

Thus, beginning rather low on this chain, you arrive at joy at last, and you get to it by the only right approach. To try to sail up to joy by the balloon of imagination is dangerous work; but to mount up to it by Jacob's ladder, every rung of which God has placed at the proper distance, is to climb to heaven by His appointed, safe road. There is nothing that the Lord Jesus says to us by way of warning that does not guard us against sorrow, conduct us away from danger, and point us to the path of safety. If we will but listen to these words of warning, they will guide us to the truest happiness that mortals can ever find either here or hereafter.

Words of Humbling

You will notice, as you read the chapter, that our Lord, in addition to words of instruction and words of warning, utters some very humbling words. I think that is a very humbling verse in which He says, *"As the branch cannot bear fruit of itself, except it abide in the vine; no more can ye, except ye abide in me"* (John 15:4). But it is good for us to be humbled and brought low. The Valley of Humiliation has always struck me as being the most beautiful place in the whole of the pilgrimage that John Bunyan described in *The Pilgrim's Progress*. What a beautiful experience it is to envision that shepherd boy, sitting down among the sheep, and to hear him playing his pipe and singing something like this:

> He that is down need fear no fall,
> He that is low no pride;
> He that is humble ever shall
> Have God to be his Guide.

This teaches us that to be brought down to our true condition of nothingness before God, to be made to feel our entire dependence upon the power of the Holy Spirit, is the true way to promote in us a joy that angels themselves might envy.

The Fullness of Joy

Therefore, beloved, be thankful whenever you read Scripture, whether it instructs you or warns you or humbles you. Say to yourself, "Somehow or other, this leads to my present and eternal joy, and therefore I will give more earnest heed to it, lest by any means I should lose the blessing it is intended to convey to me."

Words of Promise

The fifteenth chapter of John also abounds in gracious words of promise such as this: *"If ye abide in me, and my words abide in you, ye shall ask what ye will, and it shall be done unto you"* (v. 7). There are other promises here, every one of which is full of consolation to the children of God. Are any of you lacking in joy at this time? Do you feel dull and heavy of heart? Are you depressed and tried? Then listen to what Jesus Christ says here: *"These things have I spoken unto you, that my joy might remain in you, and that your joy might be full."*

What are the things that He says to you in other parts of His Word? *"Take therefore no thought for the morrow: for the morrow shall take thought for the things of itself"* (Matthew 6:34). *"Let not your heart be troubled: ye believe in God, believe also in me"* (John 14:1). *"My sheep hear my voice, and I know them, and they follow me: and I give unto them eternal life; and they shall never perish, neither shall any man pluck them out of my hand"* (John 10:27–28). In this way our Lord graciously talks to us. Do not let Him speak in vain.

My friends, do not allow His precious promises to fall upon your ears as the good seed fell upon the rocky or stony soil. The promise of harvest gives joy to the earth. Do not rob your Lord of the sheaves that He deserves to gather from your heart and life, but believe His Word, rest upon it, and rejoice in it, realizing that His words of promise are meant to bring you great joy.

Words of Precept

Christ's words of precept also bring great joy. The fifteenth chapter of John contains many of them. Jesus told us that it is His command that we should *"love one another"* (v. 12), and also that we should continue in His love (v. 9). He gave us many principles of that kind, and every precept in God's Word is a signpost pointing out the road to joy. The commandments on the tablets of stone seemed very hard, even though etched by the finger of God Himself, and the granite on which they were engraved was hard and cold. But the precepts of the Lord Jesus are tender and gracious; they bring us joy and life.

As you read these precious decrees, you may be quite sure of two things: if Christ denies you anything, it is not good for you; and if Christ commands you to do anything, obedience will promote your highest welfare.

O child of God, never quibble about any precept of your Lord! If your proud flesh should rebel, pray it down. Rest assured that, if you were so selfish as only to wish to do that which would promote your own happiness, it would be the path of wisdom to be obedient to your Lord and Master. I repeat what I wrote just above: the precepts of Christ are signposts indicating the only way to true joy. If you keep His commandments, you will abide in His love. If you carefully keep your full attention on Him in order to immediately do all that He bids you do, you will have the peace of God flowing into your soul like a river, and that peace will never fail to bring you solid and lasting joy.

PLEASING THE LORD BRINGS JOY

The next thing I gather from our text is that when our Lord Jesus Christ takes joy in us, then we also have joy. This meaning of the text is the interpretation given to it by several of the early church fathers. They have expanded our text verse, *"These things have I spoken unto you, that my joy might remain in you,"* to mean, "that I may rejoice over you, rejoice in you, and be pleased with you; thus your joy may be full." I am not certain that this is the complete meaning of the text, nor am I sure that it is not; but either way, it is a very blessed truth. Let me give you some instances to illustrate this.

A child knows that his father loves him; but while he is quite sure that his father will never cease to love him, he also knows that if he is disobedient, his father will be displeased and grieved. The obedient child gives pleasure to his father by his obedience. Moreover, when he has done so, he receives pleasure from that very fact itself.

There used to be servants in much earlier times—and I suppose there are some now—who were so attached to their masters that, if they gave satisfaction to them, they were perfectly satisfied. However, the least word of displeasure from their masters wounded them to the very heart.

Christ's Joy and Ours

Perhaps a better illustration may be found in the nearer and dearer relationship of husband and wife. The wife, if she has pleased her husband, is delighted in the joy that she has given to him; but if she has displeased him in any way, she is unhappy until she has removed the cause of his displeasure and has again given him joy.

Now, I know that my Lord Jesus loves me and that He will never do anything else but love me. Yet, He may not be always pleased with me. When He has no joy in me, my joy also dissipates if I have a heart that is true toward Him. But when He has joy in me, when He can rejoice in me, then my joy is also full. Every one of you whom the Lord has loved will find this to be true: in as much as Jesus Christ can look upon you with joy as obedient and faithful to Him, in that same proportion your conscience will be at ease, and your mind will find joy in the thought that your life is acceptable to Him.

By Abiding in Him

What are the ways in which we can really please Christ Jesus and thus have joy in Christ's pleasure? According to the chapter before us, we please Him when we abide in Him: *"If ye abide in me, and my words abide in you, ye shall ask what ye will, and it shall be done unto you"* (John 15:7). If you sometimes abide in Christ, but sometimes turn away from Him, you will give Him no pleasure. However, if He is the indispensable Companion of your daily life, if you are unhappy should the slightest cloud come between you and your Lord, if you feel that you must be as closely connected with Him as the tree limb is with the trunk or as the branch is with the stem, then you will please Him, and He will take delight in your fellowship.

Fervent love for Christ is very pleasing to Him, but the chilly, lukewarm love of Laodicea is nauseous to Him. Thus, He said, *"Because thou art lukewarm, and neither cold nor hot, I will spue thee out of my mouth"* (Revelation 3:16). Day by day, if you continue to walk with God carefully and prayerfully and to abide in Christ continually, He will look upon you with eyes of satisfaction and delight. He will see in you the reward of His sufferings. And you, being conscious that you are giving joy to Him, will find that your own cup of joy is also full to overflowing.

What greater joy can a man have than to feel that he is pleasing Christ? My fellow creatures may condemn what I do, but if Christ accepts it, it matters nothing to me how many may condemn it. They may misrepresent and misjudge me; they may impute wrong motives to me; they may sneer and snarl at me. However, if I can keep up constant and unbroken communion with the Son of God, what cause have I for sorrow? No, if He is joyful in us, then our joy will remain and will be full.

By Bringing Forth Much Fruit

Our Lord Jesus has also told us that He has joy in us when we bring forth much fruit: *"Herein is my Father glorified, that ye bear much fruit; so shall ye be my disciples"* (John 15:8). This is to say, "I will recognize in you the evidence of true discipleship with satisfaction and delight."

Beloved in Christ, are you bringing forth much fruit for God's glory? Are you called to suffer? Then, in your suffering, do you bring forth the fruit of patience? Are you strong and in robust health? Then, with that health and strength, are you rendering to the Lord the fruit of holy activity? Are you doing all you can for the Lord Jesus, who has done so much for you? You have received so much from Him; are you yielding an adequate return to Him? It is little enough when your effort is what we call very much, but how tiny it is when it is small in our own estimation!

When our Lord Jesus Christ sees us doing much for God, He is pleased with us, just as the gardener is when, having planted a tree and dug around it and fertilized it and pruned it, he sees the tree at last covered with golden fruit. The gardener is pleased with his fruitful tree, and Christ is pleased with His fruit-bearing disciples. Are we making Christ glad in this fashion? If so, our own joy will be full.

I am not surprised that some Christians have so little joy, when I remember what little pleasure they are giving to Jesus because they are producing such a sparse crop of fruit for His praise and glory. Beloved, see to this matter, I urge you. If I cannot enforce this truth with the strength that it deserves, may the power of the Holy Spirit cause the truth to come home to your hearts!

By Keeping His Commandments

In this beautiful fifteenth chapter of John, our Lord also tells us that He has joy in us when we keep His commandments:

If ye keep my commandments, ye shall abide in my love; even as I have kept my Father's commandments, and abide in his love. These things have I spoken unto you, that my joy might remain in you, and that your joy might be full. This is my commandment, That ye love one another, as I have loved you. (John 15:10–12)

The person who walks carefully in the matter of obedience to Christ's commands, wishing never to do anything offensive to Him, asking for a tender conscience so that he may be immediately aware when he is doing wrong, and earnestly desiring to leave no duty undone—such a man as that must be happy. He may not laugh much and may have very little to say when in frivolous company, but he has found a joy that foolish laughter can but mock. He has a sacred mirth within, compared to which the merriment of fools is but *"the crackling of thorns under a pot"* (Ecclesiastes 7:6). The man with a tender conscience has that joy; the careful walker has that joy. The man who, when he puts his head upon his pillow at night, can say to himself, "I have not been all that I want to be, but I have aimed at holiness; I have tried to curb my passions; I have sought to find out my Master's will and to do it in everything," sleeps sweetly. If he awakens, there is music in his heart. Whatever the trials of life may be, such a man has an abundant source of joy inside. He is pleasing to Christ. Christ has joy in him, and his joy is full.

By Loving One Another

This is especially the case with those who love others in the body of Christ. There are some who do

not love others at all; or if they do, they love themselves a great deal more. They are very apt to judge
and to condemn one another. If they can find a little
fault, they magnify it; and if they can find none, they
invent some.

I know some people who seem to be, by nature,
qualified to be monks or hermits, living quite alone.
According to their idea of things, they are much too
good for society. No church is pure enough for them;
no ministry can profit them; no one else can reach as
high as the wonderful position to which, in their
self-conceit, they imagine that they have attained.
Let none of us be of that sort. Many of the children
of God are far better than we are, and the worst one
in God's family has some points in which he is better
than we are.

Sometimes I feel as though I would give my eyes
to be as sure of heaven as the most obscure and the
least in all the family of God. I think that such times
may also come to some of you, if you imagine yourselves to be so great and good. You fat cattle, who
have pushed the lean ones with your horns and with
shoulders until the weak were scattered (Ezekiel
34:20-21), the Lord may say to you, "Go, you do not
belong to Me, for My people are not so rough and
boastful, not so proud and haughty; instead, I look to
the man who is humble, who trembles at My Word,
and who has a contrite spirit."

Did you ever try to pray to God under the influence of an awareness of possessing the higher life?
Did you ever try to pray to God that way? If you ever
did, I do not think you will do it a second time. I
tried it once, but I am not likely to repeat the ex-
periment. I thought I would try to pray to God in

that fashion, but it did not seem to come naturally from me. When I had done so, I thought I heard somebody at a distance saying, *"God be merciful to me a sinner"* (Luke 18:13), and then I saw him go home to his house justified (v. 14). Thus, I had to tear off my Pharisaic robes and get back to where the poor publican had been standing, for his place and his prayer suited me admirably.

I cannot make out what has happened to some of my family in Christ, who mistakenly believe themselves to be so wonderfully good. I wish the Lord would strip them of their self-righteousness and let them see themselves as they really are in His sight. Their fine notions concerning the higher life would soon vanish then. Beloved, the highest life I ever hope to reach, this side of heaven, is to say from my very soul,

> I the chief of sinners am,
> But Jesus died for me.

I do not have the slightest desire to suppose that I have advanced in the spiritual life many stages beyond anyone else. As long as I trust simply to the blood and righteousness of Christ and think nothing of myself, I believe that I will continue to be pleasing to the Lord Jesus Christ, that His joy will be in me, and that my joy will be full.

CHRIST'S JOY IS OURS

Now, in the third place, I think we may surmise from our text verse that the joy Jesus gives to His people is His own joy: *"That my joy might remain in you."* I venture to say that you have noticed that a man cannot communicate to another any joy except that of which he is himself conscious. A man who is rich can tell you the joy of riches, but he cannot give that joy to a poor man. Another man, who takes delight in all sorts of tomfoolery, can tell you the joy of nonsense, but he cannot make another enjoy it.

Abiding in the Father's Love

When Jesus gives us joy, He gives us His own joy. So, what do you think His joy is? First, Jesus' joy is the joy of abiding in His Father's love. He knows that His Father loves Him, that He never did anything else but love Him, that He loved Him before the earth existed, that He loved Him when He was in the manger, and that He loved Him when He was on the cross. Now, that is the joy that Christ gives to you, the joy of knowing that your heavenly Father loves you with the same kind of love.

You who really are believers in the Lord Jesus Christ ought to pause a moment and just roll that sweet morsel over your tongue—the everlasting God loves you! I have known times when I have felt as if I could leap up at the very thought of God's love for me. That He pities you and cares for you, you can understand; however, that He loves you—well, if that does not make your joy full, there is nothing that can! It ought to fill us with delight to know that we are loved by God the Father with an everlasting and infinite love, even as Jesus Christ is loved. *"The Father himself loveth you"* (John 16:27), Christ declares down through the ages. Therefore, surely you share Christ's joy, and that fact should make your own joy full.

The Fullness of Joy

Intimate Friendship

Christ's joy is also the joy of blessed friendship. He said to His disciples, *"Henceforth I call you not servants; for the servant knoweth not what his lord doeth: but I have called you friends; for all things that I have heard of my Father I have made known unto you"* (John 15:15). The friends of Jesus are those who are received by Him into a most intimate fellowship—to lean upon His breast and to become His constant companions. Our Lord Jesus Christ has great joy in being on the friendliest terms with His people. Do you not also have great joy in being on such friendly terms with Him? What higher joy do you want or could you possibly have?

I have heard a man very boastfully say that he once dined with Lord So-and-So. Another, just for the sake of showing off, spoke of his friend, Sir John Somebody-or-Other. However, you have the Lord Jesus Christ as your personal Friend, your Divine Companion. Soon you are going to sit and feast with Him at His own table. He no longer calls you His servant, but His friend. Does that fact not make you rejoice with exceeding joy? What is your heart made of, if it does not leap with joy at such an assurance as that? You are beloved of the Lord and a friend of the Son of God! Kings might well be willing to give up their crowns if they could have such bliss as this.

Glorifying the Father

Moreover, our Lord Jesus feels an intense delight in glorifying His Father. It is His constant joy to bring glory to His Father. Have you ever felt the joy of glorifying God, or do you now feel joy in Christ because He has glorified His Father? I solemnly declare that if Christ would not save me, I must still love Him for what He has done to exhibit the character of God. I have sometimes thought that if He were to shove me outdoors in the snow, I would stand there in the cold and say, "Do what You will with me; crush me if You will; but I will always love You, for there never was another such as You are, never one who so well deserved my love, and so fully won my affection and admiration as You have done."

How gloriously Christ rolled away the great load of human sin, adequately recompensed the claims of divine justice, magnified the law, and made it honorable! He took the greatest possible delight in doing this. *"For the joy that was set before him* [He] *endured the cross, despising the shame"* (Hebrews 12:2). Let that joy be yours also. Rejoice that the law is honored, that justice is satisfied, and that free grace is gloriously displayed in the atoning work of our Lord Jesus Christ.

It was Christ's joy that He glorified His Father by finishing the work that the Father had given Him to do (John 17:4). He has finished it, and therefore He is glad. Will you not also rejoice in His finished work? You do not have to sew a single stitch of the robe of righteousness that He has made. It is woven from the top throughout and absolutely perfect in every respect. You do not have to contribute even a penny to the ransom price for your redemption, for it has been paid down to the last mite.

The great redemptive work is forever finished, and Christ has done it all. He is *"Alpha and Omega, the beginning and the end"* (Revelation 21:6). He is the Author and the Finisher of our faith (Hebrews 12:2). Sit down, my brothers and sisters in Christ, and just feed on this precious truth. Surely, this is the *"feast of fat things, a feast of wines on the lees, of fat things full of marrow, of wines on the lees well refined"* (Isaiah 25:6), of which the prophet Isaiah wrote long ago.

I see You, Lord Jesus, with Your foot upon the Dragon's neck. I see You with death and hell beneath Your feet. I see the glory that adorns Your triumphant brow as You wait until the whole earth will acknowledge You as King. You have once and for all declared, *"It is finished"* (John 19:30), and finished it certainly is. My poor heart rejoices because You have finished it, and finished it for me.

CHRIST'S GIFT OF FULL, LASTING JOY

My last observation is that, when Christ communicates His joy to His people, it is a joy that remains and a joy that is full. *"These things have I spoken unto you, that my joy might remain in you, and that your joy might be full."*

A Steadfast Joy

No other joy remains like Christ's does. There is a great deal of happiness in many families when children are born, yet how many little coffins are followed by weeping mothers! There is joy when God fills the barn, and very properly so, for a bountiful harvest should make men glad; but the winter soon comes, with its cold, dark, dreary weather. But, beloved, when we receive the joy of the Lord, it stays.

Why? Because the cause of it remains. The brook will continue only as long as the spring runs, but the joy of a Christian is one that can never alter, because the cause of it never changes. God's love never changes toward His people. The Atonement never loses its efficacy. Our Lord Jesus Christ never ceases His intercession. His acceptability with God on our behalf never varies. The promises do not change. The covenant is not like the moon, sometimes waxing and sometimes waning. Oh, no, if you rejoice with Christ's joy today, you will have the same cause for rejoicing tomorrow and forever and forevermore, for He promises that His joy will remain in you.

A Fulfilling Joy

Next, this joy is full joy. Dear friends, if our joy is full, two things should be very clear to us: first, we have no room for any more joy; and, secondly, we have no room for any sorrow. When we get to know the love of God for us, we become so full of delight that we do not need or want any more joy. The pleasures of this world lose all their former charm for us.

When a man has eaten all he can eat, you may set whatever you like before him, but he has no appetite for it. "Enough is as good as a feast," we say. When a person is forgiven by God and knows that he is saved, the joy of the Lord enters his soul. That one says, "You may take all other joys and do what you like with them. I have my God, my Savior, and I want no more." Then ambition ceases, lust is quiet, covetousness is dead, and desires that once roamed abroad now stay at home. The saved one says, "My

God, You are enough for me; what more can I require? Since You have said to me, 'I love you,' and my heart has responded, 'My God, I love You, too,' I have more true wealth at my disposal than if I had all the riches of the world under my control."

There is also no longer any room for sorrow, for if Christ's joy has filled us, where can sorrow exist? "But, the man has lost all his money." "Yes," he says, "but if the Lord likes to take it from me, let Him have it." "But, the man is bereaved of those who are very dear to him, as Job was." Still, he says, *"The LORD gave, and the LORD hath taken away; blessed be the name of the LORD"* (Job 1:21). When a man consciously realizes the love of God in his soul, he cannot want more than that. I wish that all of us had that realization, because our joy would then be so great that we would have no room left for sorrow.

Now, dearly beloved, as you come to the table of your Lord in this disposition, you will feel so full of joy that you will be too full for words. People who are really full of joy do not usually talk much. A person who is carrying a glass that is full to the brim does not go dancing along like one who has nothing to carry. He is very quiet and steady, for he does not want to spill the contents of the glass. Likewise, the man who has the joy of the Lord filling his soul is often quiet; he cannot say much about it.

I have even experienced that joy to become so full that I could scarcely tell whether I was *"in the body, or out of the body"* (2 Corinthians 12:3). Pain, sickness, depression of spirit—all seem to have been taken away. I have had so clear a view of Christ, and my mind has been so separated from everything else that, afterwards, it has almost seemed like a dream to me to have felt the love of God in its almighty power, lifting me above all the surrounding circumstances.

An Unforgettable Joy

Then, dear friend, if it is so with you, the joy of the Lord will be much too full for you ever to forget it. If, at this very moment, your soul is filled with Christ's joy, it is possible that, many years from now, you may be able to say, "I remember that night twenty-three and a half years ago when I was engrossed in a book. My Lord then met with me, looked into my soul, and saw there was a void there; so He poured His own heart's joy into me until my soul could not hold any more." And, perhaps, in some dark time in the future, your present experience will be a great source of comfort to your soul. You will recall David's words in a similar circumstance: *"O my God, my soul is cast down within me: therefore will I remember thee from the land of Jordan, and of the Hermonites, from the hill Mizar"* (Psalm 42:6). You will add, "Although, now, *'deep calleth unto deep at the noise of thy waterspouts'* (v. 7), the remembrance of that bright season causes me to know that You do not forsake those on whom Your love has once been set."

An Intimate Joy

Beloved, come close to your Lord. I delight to come very near to Him. To touch the hem of His garment is enough for sinners, but it is not enough for saints. We want to sit at His feet with Mary and to lay our heads upon His bosom as John did. O you unconverted ones, look to Jesus; if you look to Him, you will live! Yet, for you who are converted, a look will not be enough for you. You want to keep on gazing at Him. You desire Him to keep gazing at you, until He says to you, *"Thou hast ravished my heart, my sister, my spouse; thou hast ravished my heart with one of thine eyes, with one chain of thy neck"* (Song 4:9). To this you will respond, *"He brought me to the banqueting house, and his banner over me was love. Stay me with flagons, comfort me with apples: for I am sick of love"* (Song 2:4).

Oh, may there now be such sweet fellowship between Christ and all His blood-besprinkled ones that, if we cannot pass the portals of heaven, we will be very near them; if we cannot hear the songs of the angels, they will at least hear ours; if we cannot look within to behold their joys, let us at least tempt them to look without to see ours. May our closeness be so dear that the angels would wish that they might be allowed to sit with us at this communion table, even though this is an honor reserved for sinners saved by sovereign grace.

> Never did angels taste above
> Redeeming grace and dying love.

May the Master smile on you, my dearly beloved, and make you to be such eminent saints that He can have great joy in you. Then, His joy will remain in you, and your joy will truly be full.

How I wish that everyone reading this knew my dear Lord and Master! I tell you who do not know Christ, and who do not experientially know what true religion is, that five minutes of the realization of the love of Christ would be better for you than a million years of your present choicest delights. There is more brightness in the dark side of Christ than in the brightest side of this poor world. I would sooner linger month after month on my bed, aching in every limb, with the sweat of death on my brow, persecuted, despised, forsaken, poor, and naked, with dogs licking my sores and demons tempting my soul, and yet have Christ for my Friend, than I would sit in the palaces of wicked kings with all their wealth and luxury and pampering and sin. Even in our lowliest state, it is better to be God's dog than the Devil's darling; it is better to have the crumbs and the moldy crusts that fall from Christ's table for the dogs than to sit at the head of princely banquets with the ungodly. *"A day in thy courts is better than a thousand* [outside]. *I had rather be a doorkeeper in the house of my God, than to dwell in the tents of wickedness"* (Psalm 84:10).

May God bless you richly. If you are still unconverted, may God have mercy on you and save you. And He will do so if you trust in Jesus Christ, His dear Son. As soon as you trust in Jesus, you are saved. May God grant that you do so this very hour, for His dear name's sake!

Chapter Five

A Wonderful Transformation

Verily, verily, I say unto you,
That ye shall weep and lament, but the world shall
rejoice: and ye shall be sorrowful,
but your sorrow shall be turned into joy.
—John 16:20

At the time Jesus said these words, our Lord was referring to His death, which He knew would cause the deepest grief to His own people, while the ungodly world would rejoice and laugh them to scorn. Thus, He implored them to look beyond the immediate present into the future and to believe that, ultimately, the cause of their sorrow would become a fountain of perpetual joy to them.

It is always wise to look a little ahead. Instead of deploring the dark clouds, let us anticipate the fruits and the flowers that will follow the descent of the needed showers. We might always be miserable if we lived only in the present, for our brightest time is yet to come. As believers in the Lord Jesus Christ, we are now only in the faint dawning of our day; the high noon will come to us by and by.

Although our Savior's words immediately related to His death, He was such a prophetic speaker that everything He said had a broader and deeper meaning than one might at first gather. Just as the fruit of the Tree of Life in the Garden of Eden foreshadows the leaves of the tree in heaven that are *"for the healing of the nations"* (Revelation 22:2), so the words of Christ, which in the past had a specific reference, now have a further living power about them. They may be applicable to present occasions instead of strictly limited to the one when they were first uttered.

Sorrow, Our Common Experience

I think I may fairly say that our Lord did not merely mean that only when He died, His children would have sorrow, but that we may take His words as a prophecy that all who truly follow Him will have their seasons of darkness and gloom. Nowhere has our Lord Jesus Christ promised to His people immunity from trial. On the contrary, He said to His disciples, *"In the world ye shall have tribulation"* (John 16:33). I cannot imagine a better promise for the wheat than that it will be threshed, and this is the promise that is made to us if we are the Lord's wheat and not the Enemy's tares:

> [Christ's] *fan is in his hand, and he will thoroughly purge his* [threshing] *floor, and gather his wheat into the garner; but he will burn up the chaff with unquenchable fire.* (Matthew 3:12)

As His wheat, you will have the threshing that will fit you for the heavenly granary. You need not mourn, beloved, that it is to be so. If you do, it will make no difference, for your Lord has declared, *"In the world ye shall have tribulation."* Be assured of that. If you could ask those believers who are now in heaven, they would tell you that they came there through great trials and tribulation. Many of them not only washed their robes in the blood of the Lamb, but they sealed their faithfulness to Him with their own blood.

EARTHLY SORROW IS GOD'S INTENTION FOR US

Our Lord intended His disciples to feel the sorrow that was to come upon them, for He said to them, *"Ye shall weep and lament,"* and He did not express any blame for their doing so. I would not have any of you even consider that there is any virtue in stoicism. I once heard a woman, wishing to show the wonders brought about in her by the grace of God, say that when her infant son died, she was so resigned to His divine will that she did not even shed a tear. However, I do not believe that it was ever God's divine will that mothers should lose their babies without shedding tears over them. I thank God that I did not have a mother who could have acted like that. I believe that as Jesus Himself wept, there can be no virtue in our saying that we do not weep.

God intends for you to feel the rod, beloved. He expects you sometimes to weep and lament, as Peter said, *"Though now for a season, if need be, ye are in heaviness through manifold temptations"* (1 Peter 1:6). That we should be in heaviness is a necessary part of our earthly discipline. Unfelt trial is no trial; certainly, it would be an unsanctified trial. Christ never meant Christians to be stoics. There is a vast difference between a gracious submission to God's divine will and a callous steeling of your heart to endure anything that happens to you without any feeling whatever. *"Ye shall be sorrowful,"* said our Lord to His disciples, and *"ye shall weep and lament."* It is through the weeping and the lamenting, oftentimes, that the very essence of the blessing comes to us.

ENDURING THE WORLD'S LAUGHTER

Our Savior mentions one aggravation of our grief, which some of us have often felt: *"the world shall rejoice."* That is the old story. David found his own trials all the harder to bear when he saw *"the prosperity of the wicked"* (Psalm 73:3). He had been plagued *"all the day long"* and *"chastened every morning"* (v. 14); he could have endured all of that if he had not seen that the ungodly had more than any heart could wish. Sometimes he found himself even troubled with the fear of death, but as for the wicked, he said,

> *There are no bands in their death: but their strength is firm. They are not in trouble as other men; neither are they plagued like other men.*
> (Psalm 73:4–5)

It makes our bitterness all the more bitter when the saints of God are afflicted, yet the enemies of God are allowed to dwell in ease. I venture to say that when you were a child, you may have fallen and hurt yourself; while you were smarting from your bruises, the other children around you were laughing at you. The pain was all the sharper because of their laughing. Likewise, the righteous are wounded to the quick when they see the ungodly prospering— prospering, apparently, because of their ungodliness. These ungodly persons will even point the finger of scorn at the righteous and ask, "Where is your God now? Is this the result of serving Him?" (Psalm 115:2).

When this is your lot, remember that your Savior told His disciples that it would be so, and He has told you the same. While you are sorrowing, you will hear their shouts of revelry. You will be up in your own room weeping, and you will hear the sound of their merry feet dizzily dancing. The very contrast between their circumstances and your own will make you feel your grief even more. Well, if this is to be our lot, we must not think it strange when it comes (1 Peter 4:12), but we may hear our Master say to us, *"But these things have I told you, that when the time shall come, ye may remember that I told you of them"* (John 16:4), and, *"If it were not so, I would have told you* [that also]*"* (John 14:2). When it happens to you, beloved, may you be able to respond, "This is just as Jesus Christ said it would be."

Christ's first disciples, if they ventured out into the streets of Jerusalem after their Savior's crucifixion while His body was in Joseph's tomb, must have found it very trying to hear the jests and jeers of those who had put the Nazarene to death. "That is the end of Him now," they cheered. "His deception is exposed, and His disciples—those poor, foolish fanatics—will soon come to their senses now, and the whole thing will collapse." That was exactly what Jesus said would happen: *"Ye shall weep and lament, but the world shall rejoice."*

GOD'S REMEDY FOR OUR SORROW

Now, what was the Savior's cure for all this? It was the fact that this trial was to last only for a little while—for a very little while. In the case of His first disciples, it was only to last for a few days, and then it would be over, for they would hear the joyful announcement, *"The Lord is risen indeed, and hath appeared to Simon"* (Luke 24:34).

So is it to be with you and with me, dear brothers and sisters in Christ. Our sorrows are all, like ourselves, mortal. There are no immortal sorrows for immortal saints. They come, but, blessed be God, they also go. Like birds of the air, they fly over our heads, but they cannot make their abode in our souls. We suffer today, but we will rejoice tomorrow. *"Weeping may endure for a night, but joy cometh in the morning"* (Psalm 30:5).

However, for that laughing sinner, what weeping and wailing will be his portion unless he repents and weeps in penitence over his many sins! The prosperity of the wicked is like a thin layer of ice on which they always stand in peril. In a moment, they may be brought down to destruction, and the place that knew them will know them no more forever. Our weeping is soon to end, but their weeping will never end. Our joy will be forever, but their joy will speedily come to an end. Look a little ahead, Christian pilgrims, for you will soon have passed through *"the valley of the shadow of death"* (Psalm 23:4). You will then come into the land where even that shadow can never fall across your pathway again.

In speaking these comforting words to His disciples, Jesus made use of this memorable sentence: *"Your sorrow shall be turned into joy."* As I read the whole passage, I pondered over those words and tried to find out their meaning. Perhaps you think, as you glance at them, that they mean that the man who was sorrowful would be joyous. That is a portion of their meaning, but they mean much more than that. They literally and actually mean exactly what is stated—your sorrow itself will be turned into joy—not your sorrow is to be taken away and joy put in its place, but rather the very sorrow that now grieves you so will be turned into joy.

GOD'S TRANSFORMATION OF SORROW INTO JOY

This is a very wonderful transformation. Only the God who works great marvels could possibly accomplish it and could, somehow, not only take away the bitterness and give sweetness in its place, but also turn the bitterness itself into sweetness.

That glorious conversion is to be the subject of our present study. I am glad to have an apt illustration of this theme in the observance of Communion, which is the highest act of Christian fellowship and unity for many of us. You know that the Lord's Supper is not at all a funeral gathering, but it is a sacred festival, in which we restfully sit, relaxing and enjoying ourselves as at a banquet. But, what are the provisions for this feast, and what do they represent? That bread, that wine—what do they mean? My friends, they represent sorrow—sorrow even unto death. The bread, apart from the wine, represents the flesh of Christ separated from His blood, and thus they set forth death. The broken bread represents the flesh of Christ bruised, marred, suffering, full of anguish. The wine represents Christ's blood poured out upon the cross, amid the agony that ended only with His death. Yet, these emblems of sorrow and suffering furnish us with our great feast of love. This is indeed joy arising out of sorrow! The festival is itself the ordained memorial of the greatest grief that was ever endured on earth. As you gather around the Lord's table, you can see in these outward emblems that sorrow is turned into joy.

OUR SORROW OVER THE LORD TURNED INTO JOY

If you will keep that picture in your mind's eye, it will help me to bring out the full meaning of the text. My first point is this: our sorrow about our blessed Lord is now turned into joy. The very things that make us grieve concerning Him are the things that make us rejoice concerning Him.

Sorrow over His Testing

This first comes to pass when we look upon Him as tempted, tried, and tested in a thousand ways. No sooner did He rise from the waters of baptism than He was led into the desert to be tempted by the Devil. We grieve to think that, for our sakes, He had to bear the brunt of a fierce duel with the Prince of Darkness. We see that He was tempted and tried and tested all His life, this way and that—sometimes by a Pharisee, sometimes by a faithless disciple. All kinds of temptations were brought to bear upon Him, for He *"was in all points tempted like as we are, yet without sin"* (Hebrews 4:15).

Joy in His Sinless Character

Yet, oh, how thankful we are to know that Christ was thus tempted, for those very temptations helped to prove the sinlessness of His character. How could we know what is in a man who has never been tested and tried? However, our Lord was tested at every point, and at no point did He fail. It is established, beyond all question or doubt, that Jesus Christ is the Lamb of God, *"without blemish and without spot"* (1 Peter 1:19).

You cannot tell what a man's strength of character is unless he is tried; there must be some process to develop the excellence that lies hidden in his nature. We ought to rejoice and bless God that our Savior was passed, like silver, through the furnace seven times (Psalm 12:6); and, like gold, He was tried again and again in the crucible, in the hottest part of the furnace. Yet, no impurity was found in Him, only the precious metal, without a particle of alloy. In this we greatly rejoice. He *"was in all points tempted like as we are, yet without sin."* He was assailed by Satan and repudiated by sinners, yet He was found faultless to the end. Thus, our joy arises out of what would otherwise have made us mourn.

Sorrow over His Sufferings

Further, beloved, remember that the griefs and trials of our Lord not only manifested His sinless

111

character, but they also made Him fit for the priestly office that He has undertaken on our behalf. The Captain of our salvation was made *"perfect through sufferings"* (Hebrews 2:10). It is necessary that He, who would truly be a benefactor to mankind, should know and understand men thoroughly. How can He sympathize with us in our sorrows unless He has, at least to some extent, felt as we do? So, our merciful and faithful High Priest is one who can be *"touched with the feeling of our infirmities"* (Hebrews 4:15), seeing that He was tempted and tried even as we are.

Joy in His Sympathetic Understanding

I think that, if I had been alive at the time and if it had been in my power, I would have spared my Lord many of his griefs, and many of you would say the same. He should have never needed to say, *"Foxes have holes, and the birds of the air have nests; but the Son of man hath not where to lay his head"* (Matthew 8:20), for you would gladly have given Him the best room in your house. Oh, but then, the poor would have missed that gracious word, which, I have no doubt, has often comforted them when they have been homeless and forlorn.

You would not have allowed Christ, if you could have helped it, to be weary and worn and hungry and thirsty. You would have liberally supplied all His needs to the utmost of your power. But, then, He would not have been so fully in sympathy as He now is with those who have to endure the direst straits of poverty, since He has passed through an experience similar to theirs. What joy it is to a hurting soul to know that Jesus has gone that way long before!

A Wonderful Transformation

I had a great grief that struck me down to the very dust, but I looked up and saw His face, which was marred more than any other. I rose to my feet in hope and joyful confidence, and I said, "Are You, my Lord, here where I am? Have You suffered thus, and did You endure far more than I can ever know of grief and brokenness of heart? Then, Savior, I rejoice and bless Your holy name." I know that you, dear friend, must have often grieved over your Savior's suffering, though you have been, at the same time, glad to remember that He passed through it all. He thus became our matchless Comforter, *"who can have compassion on the ignorant, and on them that are out of the way"* (Hebrews 5:2). Because of the very experience through which He passed, *"for in that he himself hath suffered being tempted, he is able to succour them that are tempted"* (Hebrews 2:18).

Sorrow over His Death

The meaning of our text verse comes out even more clearly when we think of the sorrows to which our Lord had been referring, which ended in His death. Oh, the griefs of Jesus when He laid down His life for His sheep! Have you not sometimes said, or at least thought, that the ransom price was too costly for such insignificant creatures as we are? Think of the agony and bloody sweat, the scourging, the spitting, the shame, the hounding through the streets, the piercing of the hands and feet, the mockery, the vinegar, the gall, the *"Eloi, Eloi, lama sabachthani?"* (Mark 15:34), and all the other horrors and terrors that gathered around the cross.

113

The Fullness of Joy

Joy in Our Salvation

We wish that they might never have happened, and yet the fact that they did happen brings to us bliss unspeakable. Our greatest joy is to know that Jesus bled and died upon the tree. How else could our sin be put away? How else could we, who are God's enemies, be reconciled and brought near to Him? How else could heaven be made for us? We might, from one aspect of Christ's sufferings, chant a mournful dirge at the foot of the cross. Yet, before we have done more than just commence the sad strain, we perceive the blessed results that come to the children of men through Christ's death. So we lay down our instruments of mourning, take up the harp and the trumpet, and sound forth glad notes of rejoicing and thanksgiving.

Joy in Christ's Wondrous Victory

Our sorrow about Christ's death is also turned into joy, not only because we derive the greatest possible benefit from it, but also because Jesus Himself, by His death, achieved such wonders.

His precious body—that fair lily, all stained with crimson stripes, from which flowed His heart's blood—must have been a pitiful sight for anyone to see. I wonder how an artist could ever paint the scenes of Christ's body being taken down from the cross or being prepared for the sepulcher. Such sorrowful sights for artists to spend themselves upon: Jesus, the final Conqueror, lying in the grave, the shroud of death wrapped about Him who once wore the purple of the universe!

However, we scarcely have time to sorrow over these facts before we recollect that the death of Christ was the death of sin; the death of Christ was the overthrow of Satan; the death of Christ was the death of death, and out of His tomb we hear that pealing trumpet note,

> *O death, where is thy sting? O grave, where is thy victory? The sting of death is sin; and the strength of sin is the law. But thanks be to God, which giveth us the victory through our Lord Jesus Christ.* (1 Corinthians 15:55–57)

I am glad that Jesus fought with Satan in the garden and vanquished him. I am glad that He fought with sin upon the cross and destroyed it. I am glad that He fought with grim death in that dark hour, and that He seized it by the throat and held it captive. I am glad that He entered the gloomy sepulcher, because He rifled it of all its terrors for His loved ones, tore its iron bars away, and set His people free. So, you see, it is all gladness, even as He said to His disciples, *"Your sorrow shall be turned into joy."*

Joy in His Glory

Whatever else there may be of sorrow that comes out of Christ's cross, we may all be glad of it, for now, Christ Himself is the more glorious because of it. It is true that nothing could add to His glory as God. However, seeing that He assumed our nature and became man as well as God, He added to His glory by all the shame He bore. There is not a reproach that pierced His heart that did not make Him more beautiful. There is not a line of sorrow that furrowed His face that did not make Him more lovely. His marred countenance is more to be admired by us than all the magnificence of earthly beauty. The Son of God was always superlatively beautiful; His beauty was such that it held the angels spellbound as they looked upon Him. The sun and moon and stars were dim compared with the brightness of His eyes. Heaven and earth could not find His equal. If all heaven had been sold, it could not have purchased this precious diamond. Yet, the setting of the diamond has made Christ appear even brighter than before—the setting of His humanity, His sufferings, His pangs, His shameful death—this setting has made His deity shine all the more resplendent. The plant that sprang from *"a root of Jesse"* (Isaiah 11:10) is now the Plant of renown. He who was despised at Nazareth is now glorified in heaven, and all the more glorified because, between Nazareth and paradise, He was *"despised and rejected of men; a man of sorrows, and acquainted with grief"* (Isaiah 53:3). Blessed Savior, we rejoice that You have gained glory by all Your sorrows, for *"wherefore God also hath highly exalted* [You], *and given* [You] *a name which is above every name"* (Philippians 2:9).

THE SORROWS OF THE CHURCH TURNED TO JOY

Now I want to remind you that, not only has Christ's suffering been turned into joy, but the sorrows of the whole church have also been turned into joy. Collectively, the members of the body of Christ have suffered greatly in order that the Gospel might be disseminated down through the ages.

A Wonderful Transformation

The Sorrows of Persecution

In speaking of the sorrows of the persecuted church of Christ, I will not compare them to the sorrows of her Lord; but if anything could be comparable to the suffering of the Bridegroom, it would be the suffering of His bride. Think of the early ages of the church of God under the Roman persecutions. Think of the church of Christ in England during the Marian persecution. My blood runs cold as I read of what the saints of God have suffered. I have often set *Foxe's Book of Martyrs* upon the shelf and thought that I could not read it any longer, because it is such an accurate account of what human nature can bear when faith in Christ sustains it.

The Joys of Honoring Christ

Yet, friends, you should not grieve that the martyrs suffered as they did. Or, if you are sorrowful, that very sorrow is turned into joy at the remembrance of how Christ has been glorified through the sufferings of His saints.

Even our poor humanity looks more lovely when we recall what it has endured for Christ's sake. When I think of the honor of being a martyr for the truth, I confess that I would sooner be in that position than be the angel Gabriel. I think it would be far better to go to heaven from the stakes than to have always been in heaven.

What honor it has brought to Christ that poor, feeble men could love Him so much that they could bleed and die for Him! Yes, and women, too, like brave Anne Askew, who, after they had racked her until they had put every bone out of joint, was still courageous enough to argue on behalf of her dear Lord. When they thought that her womanly weakness would make her back down, she seemed stronger than any man might have been. She defied them to do their worst as she said to her persecutors,

> I am not she that lists
> My anchor to let fall
> For every drizzling mist;
> My ship is substantial.

The church of God may well rejoice as she thinks of the noble army of martyrs who praise the Lord on high. Among the sweetest notes that ascend even in heaven are the songs that come from the white-robed throng who shed their blood rather than deny their Lord.

The Sorrows of Heretical Opposition

The church of Christ has also passed through fierce fires of opposition, as well as of persecution. Heresy after heresy has raged. Men have arisen who have denied one or another of the doctrines taught in the Scriptures. Every time these oppositions have come, certain feeble folk in the church have been greatly alarmed.

The Joys of the Victorious Truth

However, in looking back upon all of the heresies up to the present, I think that they are causes for joy rather than sorrow. Whenever what is supposed to be a new heresy comes up, I say to myself,

A Wonderful Transformation

"Oh, I know you; I remember reading about you. You are just an old pair of shoes, worn by heresy many hundreds of years ago, which were thrown on the trash heap. You have been picked up and cleaned up a little, and brought forth as if you were new."

I bless the Lord that, at this moment, there scarcely remains any doctrine to be defended for the first time. They have all been fought over so fiercely in the past that there is hardly any point of doctrine that our noble forefathers did not defend. Moreover, they did their work so well that we can frequently use their weapons for the defense of the truth today.

Who would wish to have kept the Word of God from going through this furnace of opposition? It is *"as silver tried in a furnace of earth, purified seven times"* (Psalm 12:6). Philosophers have tried you, O precious Book, but you were not found wanting! Atheists have tried you; sneering skeptics have tried you. They have all passed you through the fire, but not even the smell of fire is upon you to this day. In this we rejoice now and will rejoice. The day will come when the present heresies and opposition will only be recorded on the page of history as things for our successors to rejoice over, just as we now rejoice over the past victories of the truth of God.

The Sorrows and Joys of Difficult Obstacles

Once again, dear friends, not only is it so with the persecutions and oppositions of the church of Christ, but the church's difficulties have also become themes of rejoicing. As I look at the world at the present time, it does seem an impossible thing that the nations of the earth should ever be converted to

119

Christ. It is impossible as far as man alone is concerned, yet God has commanded the Christian church to evangelize the world: *"Go ye therefore, and teach all nations"* (Matthew 28:19). Someone complains that the church is too feeble and that its adherents are too few to accomplish such a task as this. The fewer the fighters, the greater their share of glory when the victory is won. In order to overcome indifference, idolatry, legalism, atheism, occultism, Hinduism, and Islam, the battle must be a very stern one, but who wants Christ's followers to fight only little battles? My brothers and sisters, let us thank God that our foes are so numerous. It matters not how many there may be of them; there are only the more to be destroyed. What did David say concerning his adversaries? *"They compassed me about; yea, they compassed me about: but in the name of the LORD I will destroy them"* (Psalm 118:11).

When the Last Day finally comes and Jehovah's banner is at last unfurled, because the book of the wars of the Lord has reached its last page, it will be a grand thing to tell the story of the whole campaign. Then it will be known to everyone that the fight for the faith was not a mere skirmish against a few feeble folk, nor was it a brief battle that began and ended in an hour, but it was a tremendous conflict *"against principalities, against powers, against the rulers of the darkness of this world, against spiritual wickedness in high places"* (Ephesians 6:12). They will have gathered together, thick as the clouds in the day of tempest, but out of heaven our Lord Himself will have thundered; He will have battled and scattered them, and they will have flown before Him *"as chaff before the wind"* (Psalm 35:5).

A Wonderful Transformation

OUR PERSONAL SORROWS TURNED INTO JOY

Now, to come down from those high themes to minor matters, our own personal *"sorrow shall be turned into joy."* When I think of the sorrows of Christ and the sorrows of His church as a whole, I say to myself, "What tiny pinpricks are our griefs compared with the great gash in the Savior's side and the many scars that adorn His church today!" But, dear friends, whatever our own sorrows may be, they will also be turned into joy.

Sometimes we are allowed to witness this wonderful transformation for ourselves. Poor old Jacob sorrowed greatly when he thought that he had lost his favorite son Joseph. When Jacob saw Joseph's coat of many colors, all torn and bloodied, he said, *"An evil beast hath devoured him; Joseph is without doubt rent in pieces"* (Genesis 37:33), and he wrung his hands and wept bitterly for many a day over his lost son. Then came the famine, and the poor old man was dreadfully alarmed concerning his large family. Jacob needed to send some of his sons into Egypt to buy food. When he sent them there, they did not all come back; Simeon had been detained as a hostage. Further, the lord of the land had said that they would not see Simeon's face again unless they brought Benjamin back with them—Benjamin, Jacob's dear and only remaining child of his beloved Rachel. He could not bear the thought of parting with Benjamin only to lose him, too. For that reason, Jacob said to his sons, *"Me have ye bereaved of my children: Joseph is not, and Simeon is not, and ye will take Benjamin away: all these things are against me"* (Genesis 42:36).

Poor Jacob, how mistaken he was! Why, all of these circumstances were as favorable for him as they could possibly be. His dear Joseph, down in Egypt, was sitting next to Pharaoh on the throne, ready to provide for his father and all of the family during the time of famine. Then, there was the famine itself that made Jacob send down to Egypt. Because of the famine, Jacob found out that Joseph was still alive, journeyed and saw his face again, and confessed that the Lord had dealt graciously with him (Genesis 33:11). You dear children of God, who fret and are troubled, should carry out Cowper's good advice:

> Judge not the Lord by feeble sense,
> But trust Him for His grace;
> Behind a frowning providence
> He hides a smiling face.

You have quite enough to cry over without fretting concerning things that you will rejoice over someday. The Lord will put your tears into His bottle (Psalm 56:8); when He shows them to you by and by, I think you will say, "How foolish I was ever to shed them, because the very thing I wept over was really a cause for rejoicing, if I could have only seen a little way ahead." It is like that sometimes in God's providence, as you will discover over and over again between here and heaven.

Our Sorrows Drive Us to God

Our sorrows, dear friends, are turned into joy in many different ways. For instance, there are some of us who are such independent, thoughtless children that we never seem to come close to our heavenly Father unless some sorrow drives us to Him. We ought to be more with Him in days of sunshine, if possible, than in days of storm, but it is not always so. It is said that the more you whip some dogs, the more they love you. I should not like to try that plan even on a dog, but I fear that some of us are very much like dogs in that respect, if the saying is true. When we have a great trouble or get a sharp cut, we seem to wake up and say, "O Lord, I forgot You when all was going smoothly; I wandered from You then, but now I must come back to You."

We often develop a special softness of heart and mellowness of spirit only through being tried and troubled. When that is the case, you and I have great cause to rejoice in our sorrows. They draw us nearer to God and bring us into a closer and more careful walk with Him. When they draw us away from self-complacency and self-sufficiency and worldliness, our sorrows are immediately turned into joy— if we are wise men and women.

Our Sorrows Reveal God's Promises

Again, there is no doubt that, to many, sorrow is a great means of opening the eyes to the preciousness of the promises of God. I believe that we will never get to know the meaning of some of God's promises until we have been placed in the circumstances for which those promises were written. Certain objects in nature can only be seen from certain points of view, and there are precious things in the covenant of grace that can only be perceived from the deep places of trouble. Well, then, if your trouble brings you into a position where you can understand more of the lovingkindness of the Lord, you will be very thankful that you were ever put there, for you will thus find your sorrow turned into joy.

Sorrow Brings Us into Deeper Fellowship

Again, sorrow often gives us further fellowship with Christ. There are times when we can say, "Now, Lord, we can sympathize with You better than we ever did before, for we have felt somewhat as You did in Your agony here below." We have sometimes felt as though that prophecy had been fulfilled to us, *"Ye shall drink indeed of my cup, and be baptized with the baptism that I am baptized with"* (Matthew 20:23). For instance, if friends forsake you, if he who eats bread with you turns against you, you can say, "Now, Lord, I know a little better what You felt when Judas so basely betrayed You." You cannot so fully comprehend the griefs of Christ unless, in your humble measure, you have to pass through a somewhat similar experience. However, when you perceive that you can sympathize more with Christ because of your own sorrow, then, certainly your sorrow is turned into joy.

Sorrows Make Us Partners with Christ

Sorrow also gives us fellowship with our Lord in another way: we feel as if we have become partners with Christ in our trials. Here is a cross, and I have to carry one end of it. However, I look around and see that my Lord is carrying the heavier end of it. Then it is a very sweet sorrow to carry the cross in partnership with Christ. Rutherford wrote in one of his letters, "When Christ's dear child is carrying a burden, it often happens that Christ says, 'Halves, My love,' and carries half of it for him." It is indeed sweet when it is so.

If there is a ring of fire on your finger, and that ring means that you are married to Christ, you may well be willing to wear it no matter what suffering it may cause you. Those were blessed nails that fastened you to the cross, even though they were nails of iron that went right through your flesh, for they kept you all the closer to your Lord.

Our motto must be, "Anywhere with Jesus; nowhere without Jesus." Anywhere with Jesus? Yes, even into Nebuchadnezzar's furnace. When we have the Son of God with us, the glowing coals cannot hurt us. They become a bed of roses to us when He is there. Where Jesus is, our sorrow is turned into joy.

Sorrows of Death Swallowed Up in Victory

I must not fail to remind you that there is a time coming when *"the sorrows of death"* (Psalm 18:4) will get a grip on us. I want you, brothers and sisters, to understand that, unless the Lord comes first, we will not escape the sorrow of dying, but it will be turned into joy. It has been my great pleasure to see many Christians in their last moments on earth, and I am sure that the merriest people I have ever seen have been dying saints. I have been to wedding feasts. I have seen the joy of young people in their youth. I have seen the joy of the merchant when he has made a prosperous venture. I have myself experienced joys of various kinds, but I have never seen any joy that I have so envied as that which has sparkled in the eyes of departing believers.

Just now, there rises up in my mind's eye a vision of the two eyes of a poor consumptive girl—oh, how bright they were! I heard that she was close to death's door, so I went to try to comfort her. To comfort her? Oh, dear, she needed no comforting from me! Every now and then, she would burst forth into a verse of sacred song; and when she stopped, she would tell me how precious Jesus was to her, what loving visits He had already paid her, and how soon she expected to be forever with Him. There was not, in all the palaces of Europe or in all the mansions of the wealthy or in all the ballrooms of the affluent, such a merry and joyous spirit as I saw shining through the bright eyes of that poor shadow of a girl, who had very little here below, but who had so much laid up for her in heaven that it did not matter what she had here. Yes, beloved, your sorrow will be turned into joy.

Many of you will not even know that you are dying. You will shut your eyes on earth and open them in heaven. Some of you may be dreading death, for there is still a measure of unbelief remaining in you. But, in your case also, *"death* [will be] *swallowed up in victory"* (1 Corinthians 15:54). Just as when some people have to take very bitter medicine, it is put into some sweet liquid, and they drink it down without tasting the bitterness, so will it be with all of us who are trusting in the Lord Jesus Christ when we have to drink our last potion. In a few more days or weeks or months or years—it does not matter which, for it will be a very short time at the most—all of us who love the Lord will be with

Him where He is, to behold His glory and to share it with Him forever.

Have any of you any sorrows that you still wish to talk about? Some of you are very poor, and others of you are very much tried and troubled in many ways. But, my dear friends, when you and I get to heaven—and we will all do so before long—I think you will have the best of it. If there is any truth in that line, "The deeper their sorrows, the louder they'll sing," the more sorrows you have had, the more you will sing. Nobody enjoys wealth like a man who has been poor. Nobody enjoys health like a man who has been sick. I think that the most pleasant days I ever spend are those that follow a long illness, when I at last begin to go outside and drink in the sweet, fresh air again. And, oh, what joy it will be to you poor ones and you sick ones and you tried ones to get into the land where all is plentiful, where all is peaceful, where all is joyful, where all is holy! You will be there soon—some of you will be there very soon. Dr. Watts penned it this way:

> There, on a green and flowery mount,
> Our weary souls shall sit,
> And with transporting joys recount
> The labors of our feet.

This simply means that the very sorrows we pass through in our earthly pilgrimage will constitute topics for joyful conversation in heaven. I do not doubt that it will be so. In heaven, we will be as glad of our troubles as of our mercies. Perhaps then it will appear to us that God never loved us so much as when He chastened and tried us. When we get home to glory, we will be like children, having grown up and matured, who sometimes say to a wise parent, "Father, I have forgotten about the holidays you gave me; I have forgotten about the pocket money you gave; I have forgotten about a great many sweet things that I very much liked when I was a child; but I have never forgotten the whipping that you gave me when I did wrong, for it altogether saved me from turning out badly. Dear father, I know you did not like to do it, but I am very grateful to you for it now—more grateful for that whipping than for all the candy and treats that you gave me." Likewise, when we get home to heaven, I have no doubt that we will feel, and perhaps say, "Lord, we are grateful to You for everything, but most of all for our sorrows. We see that had You left us unchastised, we would never have been what we now are. Thank You, for You have turned our sorrows into joy."

As for you who are not believers in the Lord Jesus Christ, I want you to ponder most solemnly these few words and to carry them with you in your heart. If you remain as you are, your joys will be turned into sorrows. God grant that they may not be, for Jesus Christ's sake!

Chapter Six

A Harp of Ten Strings

And Mary said, My soul doth magnify the Lord, and
my spirit hath rejoiced in God my Saviour.
For he hath regarded the low estate of his
handmaiden: for, behold, from henceforth all
generations shall call me blessed.
For he that is mighty hath done to me great things;
and holy is his name. And his mercy is on them that
fear him from generation to generation. He hath
showed strength with his arm; he hath scattered the
proud in the imagination of their hearts. He hath put
down the mighty from their seats, and exalted them
of low degree. He hath filled the hungry with good
things; and the rich he hath sent empty away.
He hath holpen his servant Israel, in remembrance of
his mercy; as he spake to our fathers, to Abraham,
and to his seed for ever.
—Luke 1:46–55

I t seems very clear in this passage that Mary was
not beginning a new behavior, for she spoke in
the present tense, in a tense that seems to have
been present for some time in her life: *"My soul doth*

magnify the Lord." Ever since she had received the wonderful tidings that God had chosen her for the high position of being the mother of the Messiah, she had begun to magnify the Lord.

When once a soul has a deep sense of God's mercy and begins to magnify Him, there is no end to his worship. It grows by what it feeds upon: the more you magnify God, the more you can magnify Him. The higher you live, the more you can see. Your view of God is increased in its extent. Where before you praised Him a little at the bottom of the hill, when you get nearer to the top of His exceeding goodness, you lift up the strain still more loudly, and your soul more fully and exultantly magnifies the Lord.

THE MEANING OF MAGNIFICATION

"My soul doth magnify the Lord." What does it mean? The usual signification of the word *magnify* is to make great or to make to appear great. We say that when we use a microscope, it magnifies so many times. The insect is the same small, tiny thing, but it is increased in size in our apprehension.

The word *magnify* is also very suitable in our present situation. We cannot make God greater than He is, nor can we have any conception of His actual greatness. He is infinitely above our highest thoughts. When we meditate upon His attributes,

> Imagination's utmost stretch
> In wonder dies away.

We magnify our Lord by having higher, larger, truer conceptions of Him—by making known His mighty acts and praising His glorious name—so that others, too, may exalt Him in their thoughts. This is what Mary was doing: she was a woman who was given to pondering. Those who heard what the shepherds said concerning the holy child Jesus wondered, but *"Mary kept all these things, and pondered them in her heart"* (Luke 2:19). They wondered; Mary pondered. It is only the change of a letter, but it makes a great difference in the attitude of the soul, a change from a vague flash of interest to a deep attention of heart. She pondered: she weighed the matter; she turned it over in her mind; she thought about it; she estimated its value and result. She was like that other Mary, a meditative woman who quietly waited at her Lord's feet to hear His gracious words and to drink them in with yearning faith.

It is no idle occupation thus to get alone, and in your own heart, to magnify the Lord: to make Him great to your mind, to your affections; great in your memory, great in your expectations. It is one of the grandest exercises of the renewed nature. You need not, at such a time, think of the deep questions of Scripture. You may leave the complex doctrines to wiser minds, if you will.

However, if your very soul is bent on making God great in your own comprehension, you will be spending time in one of the most profitable ways possible for a child of God. Depend upon it, there are countless holy influences that flow from the habitual maintenance of great thoughts of God, just as there are incalculable mischiefs that flow from our small thoughts of Him. The root of false theology is belittling God, and the essence of true divinity is enhancing God, magnifying Him, and enlarging our concepts of His majesty and His glory to the utmost.

Yet, Mary did not mean, by magnifying the Lord, merely to extol Him in her own thoughts. Being a true poetess, she intended to magnify the Lord by her words. No, I must correct that—she did not intend to do it, she had been doing it all along. She was doing it when she came, panting and breathless, into her cousin Elizabeth's house. She said, *"'My soul doth magnify the Lord.'* I am now in such a favored condition that I cannot open my mouth to talk to you, Elizabeth, without speaking of my Lord. My soul now seems filled with thoughts of Him. I must speak, first of all, about Him, and say such things of His grace and power as may help you, my godly older sister, still to think even grander thoughts of God than you have ever before enjoyed. *'My soul doth magnify the Lord.'"*

MARY'S HUMILITY

We must recall the fact that Mary was highly distinguished and honored. No other woman was ever blessed as she was; perhaps no other could have borne the honor that was put upon her—to be the mother of the human nature of our Savior. It was the highest possible honor that could be put upon mortal flesh. At the appointed time, the Lord knew where to find a guileless, lowly woman who could be entrusted with such a gift and yet not seek to pilfer away His glory. She was not proud; no, it is a false heart that steals the revenues of God and buys the intoxicating cup of self-congratulation with the looted gain.

The more God gives to a true heart, the more that heart gives back to Him. Like Peter's boat,

which sank more deeply in the water, the more fully
it was laden with fish, God's true children sink in
their own esteem as they are honored by their Lord.
God's gifts, when He gives grace with them, do not
puff us up; rather, they build us up.

A humble and lowly estimate of ourselves is
added when we have a greater esteem of our Lord.
The more God gives you, the more you should magnify Him and not yourself. This should be your rule:
"He must increase, but I must decrease" (John 3:30).
Become less and less. Be the Lord's humble servant,
yet be bold and confident in your praise of Him who
has done great things for you. Henceforth and forever, let this be the one description of your life: *"'My
soul doth magnify the Lord.'* I have nothing else to
do anymore but to magnify Him and to rejoice in
God my Savior."

MARY'S SONG

An entire book might be profitably produced
were I to attempt to teach about each part of Mary's
song; but with quite another purpose in mind, I am
going to present it to you as a whole. As I put before
you this instrument of ten strings, I will ask you,
just for a moment or two, to place your fingers on
each of the strings as they are indicated. See if you
can wake some melody to the praise of the great
King, some harmony in His honor. Discover if you
can, right now, how to magnify the Lord and rejoice
in God your Savior.

Martin Luther used to say that the glory of
Scripture was to be found in the pronouns; this is
certainly true of our text. Look at the personal touch

of them, how it comes over and over again! *"My soul doth magnify the Lord, and my spirit hath rejoiced in God my Saviour."* At a festival at our orphanage, I gave our many friends who were gathered there several reasons why everyone should contribute to the support of the children. "Indeed," I said, "nobody ought to go off the grounds without giving something." I was struck with one brother, who had no money with him, but who brought me his watch and chain. "Oh," I said, "do not give me these things, for they will sell for so little compared with their value." However, he insisted upon my keeping them and said, "I will redeem them tomorrow, but I cannot go away without giving something now."

How glad I would be if every child of God should be as earnest in adoration! As we enter our churches to worship, if only we could say, "I am going to give some praise to God at this service: out of some of those strings I will get music, perhaps out of them all. I will endeavor with my whole heart to say, at some portion of the service and from some point of view, *'My soul doth magnify the Lord'*!"

Do I hear you whisper, "My soul is very heavy"? Lift it up, then, by praising the Lord; begin a psalm, even if at first the tune must be in a minor key. Soon the strain will change, and the "Miserere" will become a "Hallelujah Chorus."

THE FIRST STRING OF JOY

The first string that Mary seemed to touch—and that, I trust, we may also reach with the hand of faith—is that of the great joy to be found in the Lord. *"My soul doth magnify the Lord, and my spirit*

hath rejoiced in God my Saviour." Let us bless God
that our religion is not one of gloom. I do not know
of any commandment anywhere in Scripture that
says, "Groan in the Lord always, and again I say,
Groan." From the morose conduct of some Christians, we might surmise that they must have altered
their New Testaments in that particular passage and
thus woefully changed the glory of the original verse:
"Rejoice in the Lord alway: and again I say, Rejoice"
(Philippians 4:4).

The first I ever truly knew of my Master was
when I found myself at the foot of His cross, with
the great burden that had crushed me effectually
gone. I looked around for it, wondering where it
could be, and, behold, it was tumbling down into His
sepulcher. I have never seen it since, blessed be His
name, nor do I ever want to see it again! Well do I
remember the leaps of joy I did when I first found
that all my burden of guilt had been borne by Him
and was buried in the depths of His grave.

> Many days have passed since then;
> Many changes I have seen!

I have been to many different wells to find water, but when I have drawn and tasted from them,
the liquid has been as brackish as the waters of
Marah. Yet, whenever I have gone to this well—
"God my Saviour"—I have never drawn one drop
that was not sweet and refreshing. He who truly
knows God must be glad in Him. To abide in His
house is to be praising Him continually. Yes, we may
rejoice in Him all the day long.

A very notable word is that which was found in
the mouth of David: *"God my exceeding joy"* (Psalm

43:4). Other things may give us pleasure; we may be happy in the gifts of God and in His creatures, but God Himself, the Spring of all our joys, is greater than them all. Therefore, *"Delight thyself also in the LORD"* (Psalm 37:4). This is His command, and is it not a lovely one? Let no one say that the faith of the Christian is not to be exultant. It is to be a delight. So greatly does God desire us to rejoice in Him that to the command is added a promise: *"and he shall give thee the desires of thine heart."*

What a faith is ours, in which delight becomes a duty, in which to be happy is to be obedient to a command! Heathen religions exact not only self-denials of a proper kind and form, but tortures that men invent to accustom themselves to misery. However, in our holy faith, if we keep close to Christ, while it is true that we bear the cross, it is also true that the cross ceases to be a torture. In fact, it often bears us as we bear it. We discover in the service of our Master that His *"yoke is easy, and* [His] *burden is light"* (Matthew 11:30), and that, strange to say, His burden gives us rest, and His yoke gives us liberty. We have never had anything from our Master that has not ultimately led to our joy. Even when His rod has made us wince, He has intended it to work for our good, and such good it has produced. Praise Him, then, for such goodness.

Our faith is one of holy joy, especially regarding our Savior. The more we understand that glorious word *Savior,* the more are we ready to dance with delight. *"My spirit hath rejoiced in God my Saviour."* The good tidings of great joy have reached us; as we, by His grace, have believed them, He has saved us from sin and death and hell. He has not simply promised to do it someday, but He has already done it; we have been saved. Moreover, so many of us have entered into rest by faith in Him; salvation is to us a present experience at this very hour, although we still wait for the fullness of it to be revealed in the world to come.

Oh, come, let us rejoice in our Savior. Let us thank Him that we have so much for which to thank Him. Let us praise Him that there is so much that we may rejoice in, so much that we *must* rejoice in. Let us adore His dear name. Let us delight in the knowledge that He has so arranged the whole plan of salvation, that it is calculated to bring heaven to us while we are here and to bring us who are here into heaven hereafter. Therefore, we lift up our hearts because of the great joy that is laid up for us in God.

This is the first string of your heavenly harp. Touch it now. Think of all the joy you have had in God. Praise Him for all the holy mirth He has given you in His house, the bliss of communion with Him at His table, the delights of fellowship with Him in secret. Sing to Him with a grateful heart, saying, *"My soul doth magnify the Lord."*

THE SECOND STRING OF CHRIST'S DEITY

The second string we desire to lay our fingers upon is the Godhead of our Savior. *"My soul doth magnify the Lord."*

I do not have a little Lord. *"And my spirit hath rejoiced in God my Saviour."* I know that Jesus Christ is a man, and I rejoice in His humanity. But I will contend to the death for this truth: He is more than man, He is our Savior. One human being could not redeem another or give to God a ransom for his brother. An angel's arm could not bear the tremendous load of the disaster of the Fall, but Christ's arm is more than angelic. He whom we magnify as our Savior, *"being in the form of God, thought it not robbery to be equal with God"* (Philippians 2:6). When He undertook the wondrous task of our redemption, He brought the Godhead with Him to sustain Him in that more than Herculean labor: *"For in him dwelleth all the fulness of the Godhead bodily"* (Colossians 2:9).

Our trust is in Jesus Christ, very God of very God. We will never cease, not only to believe in Him, but also to speak of Him, rejoice in Him, and sing of Him as the incarnate Deity. What a frozen religion it is that does not have the Godhead of Christ in it! Surely, men who can pretend to receive any comfort out of a faith that does not have the divine Savior as its very center must be of a very self-assured and imaginative temperament. I would just as soon consider going to an iceberg to warm myself as to a religion of that kind to find comfort. Nobody can ever magnify Christ too much for me, nor can they say too much in praise of His wisdom or of His power. Every divine attribute ascribed to Christ makes me lift up a new song to Him; for, whatever He may be to others, to me He is God *"who is over all, God blessed for ever"* (Romans 9:5).

I wish that I could sing these words instead of writing them—words about God the Son who was with the Father before all worlds began; whose delights, even then, were with the sons of men in the prospect of their creation. I wish that I could tell the wonderful story of how our Savior entered into covenant with God on the behalf of His people and pledged Himself to pay the debts of those His Father gave to Him. He undertook to gather into one fold all the sheep whom He promised to purchase with His own precious blood. He contracted to bring them back from all their wanderings and draw them together to graze on the hilltops of the Delectable Mountains at His Father's feet. This He vowed to do, and He has gone about His task with a zeal that has clothed him as a cloak. Moreover, He will achieve the divine purpose before He delivers up the kingdom to God, even the Father. *"He shall not fail nor be discouraged"* (Isaiah 42:4).

It is our delight to hear this Son of God, this wondrous Being in His complex nature as our Mediator, exalted and extolled and very highly elevated. Have you not sometimes felt that if your minister preached more about Jesus Christ, you would be very glad to hear him? I hope that is your inclination, yet I am afraid that we talk a great deal about many things rather than about our Master. Come, let me hear of Him; sing to me or talk to me of Jesus, whose name is honey in the mouth, music in the ear, and heaven in the heart. Oh, for more praise of His holy name! Yes, some of us can touch this string and sing with Mary, *"My soul doth magnify the Lord, and my spirit hath rejoiced in God my Saviour."*

THE THIRD STRING OF JESUS' CONDESCENSION

The third string has softer, sweeter music in it, and it may suit some of us better than the more sublime themes that we have already touched. Let us sing and magnify the Lord's loving condescension, just as Mary did when she went on to say, *"For he hath regarded the low estate of his handmaiden."* Here is something to sing about, for ours was not only a low estate, but perhaps some would have had to say, like Gideon, *"My family is poor...and I am the least in my father's house"* (Judges 6:15). Like him, you would have been passed over by most people. Possibly even in your own family, you were considered a nobody: if someone uttered a jest, you were sure to be the butt of it; and generally you were misunderstood and your actions misinterpreted. This was a trying experience for you, but from this you have been gloriously delivered. It may have been that, like Joseph, you were a little dreamy, and perhaps you were a trifle too fond of telling your dreams. Yet, though you were much ridiculed because of this, the Lord at length raised your head up above those around you. It may have been that your lot in life was cast among the very poorest and lowest of mankind, yet the Lord has looked upon you in infinite compassion and saved you. Will you not, then, magnify Him?

If Christ wanted a special people, why did He not choose the kings and princes and nobles of the earth? Instead of them, He takes the poor and makes them to know the wonders of His dying love. Instead of selecting the wisest men in the world, He takes even the most foolish and instructs them in the things of the kingdom.

> Wonders of grace to God belong,
> Repeat His mercies in your song.

All of us who have been saved by grace must strike an even tenderer note, for we were sinful as well as lowly. We went astray like lost sheep; we therefore magnify the Lord, who bought us and sought us and brought us back to His fold. It may be painful to remember what we once were, but it is good sometimes to go back in our thoughts to the time past when we lived in sin, in order that we may better appreciate the favor of which we have been made partakers.

When the apostle Paul wrote out a register of those who will not inherit the kingdom of God, he added, *"And such were some of you: but ye are washed, but ye are sanctified, but ye are justified in the name of the Lord Jesus, and by the Spirit of our God"* (1 Corinthians 6:11). Oh, let us bless the name of the Lord and magnify Him for this! Who else could have cleansed us from our sin? In what other fountain except the one open to the house of David could we have plunged to rid us of our awful defilement?

Christ stoops very low, for some of God's elect were once the most contemptible outcasts. Even when converted, many remained so in the estimate of the world, which sneers at humble Christians. If the followers of Christ happen to meet in some fine building and worship God with grand music and gorgeous ritual, then the people of the world put up with them. They may go even so far as to patronize them, although, even then, their respect is chiefly aroused, not on behalf of the people, but because of the fine building, the artistic music, and the caliber of the transportation. Quality vehicles are especially important to the world, for without a certain number of them parked in front of the church edifice, it is deemed utterly impossible to have a proper display of cultured Christianity.

The more God's people cling to the Lord, the less likely they are to be esteemed highly in the vulgar judgment of unholy men. Yet, the Lord has chosen people of such lowly estate, blessed be His name! It is a great wonder to me that the Lord ever chose some of you, but it is a far greater wonder that He should ever have chosen me! I can somehow understand His love for you, when I look at the gracious points in your character—although I am fully aware that they are only wrought by His grace—but I cannot begin to comprehend the love that He has displayed *"unto me, who am less than the least of all saints"* (Ephesians 3:8). You are probably thinking, "Oh! That is what I was going to say about myself." Yes, I know. I am trying to put it into your mind, so that we may all join in adoring gratitude. It is a miracle of mercy that He should have loved any of us, or that He stooped in His grace to raise such beggars from the dunghill to set us among the princes at His right hand (1 Samuel 2:8).

> Why was I made to hear Thy voice,
> And enter while there's room;
> When thousands make a wretched choice,
> And rather starve than come?

THE FOURTH STRING OF GOD'S GOODNESS

The next string, however, is the greatness of God's goodness, for Mary continued to sing: *"He hath regarded the low estate of his handmaiden: for, behold, from henceforth all generations shall call me blessed."* Oh, the Lord has done great things for His people! *"He that is mighty hath done to me great things; and holy is his name."*

142

God has made you blessed. You were once under the curse, but *"there is therefore now no condemnation* [for you who] *are in Christ Jesus"* (Romans 8:1). If He had allowed the curse to wither you like some lightning-blasted oak, you could not have questioned it. However, the gracious Lord has instead planted you by the rivers of water; He causes you to bring forth fruit in your season and your leaf not to wither (Psalm 1:3). *"The LORD hath done great things for us; whereof we are glad"* (Psalm 126:3).

To be lifted up from that *"horrible pit, out of the miry clay"* (Psalm 40:2), is such a great thing that we cannot measure it, but to be set upon that throne of mercy in Christ Jesus exceeds our highest thought. Who can measure that? Take your measuring line, and see if you can fathom the depth of such grace or gauge the height of such mercy. Will we be silent when we behold such marvelous lovingkindness? God forbid it! Let us break forth in our hearts now with joyous hallelujahs to Him who has done such wonderful things for us!

Think, beloved! You were blind, but He has made you see. You were lame, but He has made you leap. Worse than that, you were dead, but He has made you live. You were in prison, but He has set you free. Some of us were in the dungeon, with our feet fast in the stocks. Can I not well remember when I was bound in that inner prison, moaning and groaning, without any voice to comfort me or even a ray of light to cheer me in the darkness? And now that He has brought me out, will I forget to utter my deepest thanks? No, I will sing *"songs of deliverance"* (Psalm 32:7), so that others may hear and fear and turn unto the Lord.

Yet, that is not all our Lord has done. He has not only released us from the prison, but He has also seated us in heavenly places (Ephesians 2:6). You and I could go into heaven tonight, if God called us there, and every angel would treat us with respect. If we entered into paradise, even though we had come from the poorest home in the city, we would find that the highest angels are only ministering servants to the chosen people of God. Oh, He has done wonders for us!

I am very much attempting to awaken your memories, so that you may think of the goodness of the Lord's grace and say, "Oh, yes, it is so, and *'my soul doth magnify the Lord'*!"

Not one of the wonders of divine grace has been produced for us without deep necessity for its manifestation. If the very least grace, which may have escaped your attention previously, were taken from you, where would you be? I often meet with people of God who used to be very happy and joyful, but who have fallen into despondency, and who now talk about the mercies of God's covenant love in such a way as to make me blush. They say, "I thought I once had that blessing, but I am afraid I do not have it now, although there is nothing I long for more. Oh, what a precious thing it would be to be able to have access to God in prayer! I would give my eyes to be able to know that I am really a child of God."

Yet, those of us who have these blessings do not often value them; no, dear friends, we do not value them a thousandth part as much as we ought. Our constant song should be: *"Blessed be the Lord, who daily loadeth us with benefits, even the God of our salvation"* (Psalm 68:19). Instead of that, we often take the gifts thoughtlessly and ungratefully from His hand. When a man has plunged himself underwater to the depths of the sea, he may have a great deal of water over his head and not feel it. Yet, when he comes out, if you then put a little pail of water on his head, it becomes quite a burden to him as he carries it. Likewise, some of you are swimming in God's mercy. You are diving into it, and you do not recognize the weight of the glory that God has bestowed upon you. But, if you should once get out of this ocean of joy and fall into a state of sadness of heart, you would begin to appreciate the weight of any one of the mercies, which now do not seem to be of much consequence or to make any claim upon your gratitude. Without waiting to lose the sense of God's grace, in order that we may know the value of it, let us bless Him who has done such inconceivably great things for us. Let us declare, *"My soul doth magnify the Lord."*

THE FIFTH STRING OF HIS GRACE AND HOLINESS

The fifth string that I would touch is the combination of grace and holiness that we find in what God has done for us: *"He that is mighty hath done to me great things; and holy is his name."* I may not even hint at the particular delicacy of Mary's case, but she knew that it was wholly holy and pure. Now, when the Lord has saved us who did not deserve saving, He did a very wonderful act of sovereign grace in changing us, but the mercy is that He did it all justly.

Nobody can ever say that our salvation ought not to have been bestowed on us. At the Last Great

Day, what God has done in His grace will stand the test of justice, for He has never, in the splendor and lavishness of His love, violated the principles of eternal righteousness, even to save His own elect. *"He that is mighty hath done to me great things; and holy is his name."* Sin must be punished: it has been punished in the person of our glorious Substitute. No man can enter into heaven unless he is perfectly pure. They who are redeemed can take no unclean thing within the gates. Every rule and mandate of the divine empire must be observed. The Lawmaker will not be a lawbreaker even to save the sinner. His law will be honored as surely as the sinner will be saved.

Sometimes I feel that I could play on this harp string for hours. Here we have justice, magnified in grace and holiness, rejoicing in the salvation of sinners. The attributes of God are like the clear white light shining through a crystal prism, which may yet be divided into all the colors of the spectrum, each different and all beautiful. The dazzling radiance of God is too glorious for our mortal eyes, but each revelation teaches us more of His beauty and perfectness. In the ruby light of Christ's atoning sacrifice, we are enabled to see how God is just and yet the Justifier of him who believes in Jesus. Glory be to His name for the power of grace mingled with holiness!

"My soul doth magnify the Lord" for this wonderful salvation, in which God's every attribute has its glory—justice as well as mercy, wisdom as well as might. *"Mercy and truth are met together; righteousness and peace have kissed each other"* (Psalm 85:10). Who could have invented such a plan, and

who could have carried it out when it was thought of? Only our wonderful Savior and Lord. *"My soul doth magnify the Lord, and my spirit hath rejoiced in God my Saviour."*

THE SIXTH STRING OF GOD'S MERCY

The sixth string is one that should be sweet in every way. Mary went on to touch the string of God's mercy. *"And his mercy is on them that fear him."* The saints of old often touched this string in the temple. They often sang it, lifting up the refrain again and again: *"His mercy endureth for ever"* (Psalm 136:1).

> For His mercy shall endure,
> Ever faithful; ever sure.

Mercy! Sinner, this is the silver bell for you: *"It is of the LORD'S mercies that* [you] *are not consumed, because his compassions fail not"* (Lamentations 3:22). Listen to the heavenly music that calls you to repent and live. God delights in mercy. He waits to be gracious. Mercy! Saint, this is the golden bell for you, for you still need mercy. Standing with your foot upon the jasper doorstep of paradise, with the pearly gate just before you, you will still need mercy to help you over the last step. When you enter the choir of the redeemed, mercy will be your perpetual song. In heaven you will chant the praises of the God of grace, whose *"mercy endureth for ever."*

Do you mourn over your own backsliding? God will have mercy upon you, dear child, even though you have wandered since you have known Him. Come back to Him this very hour. He wants to woo you again. He wants to press you to His bosom. Have you not often been restored? Have you not often had your iniquities put away from you in the years gone by? If so, again touch this string—a child's finger can make it bring forth its music—touch it now. Say, "Yes, concerning mercy, mercy to this very chief of sinners, *'my soul doth magnify the Lord, and my spirit hath rejoiced in God my Saviour.'*"

THE SEVENTH STRING OF GOD'S IMMUTABILITY

Space would fail me if I tried to dwell at any length upon any one these wondrous themes, and so I will pass to the next string, number seven, God's immutability. In the verse we have already touched upon, there are two notes, one of His mercy and one of this melody. Mary said, *"His mercy is on them that fear him from generation to generation."* He who had mercy in the days of Mary has mercy today: *"from generation to generation."* He is eternally the same God. *"I am the LORD, I change not; therefore ye sons of Jacob are not consumed"* (Malachi 3:6). You that once delighted in the Lord, do not suppose that He has altered. He still invites you to come and delight in Him. He is *"Jesus Christ the same yesterday, and to day, and for ever"* (Hebrews 13:8).

What a poor foundation we would have for our hope if God could change! But He has confirmed His word by an oath, *"that by two immutable things, in which it was impossible for God to lie, we might have a strong consolation, who have fled for refuge to lay hold upon the hope set before us"* (Hebrews 6:18). The God of my grandfather, the God of my father, is my God this day. The God of Abraham, Isaac, and

Jacob is the God of every believer. He is the same God; He is prepared to do the same and to be the same to us as to them. Look back into your own experience; have you not found God always the same? Come, protest against Him if you have ever found Him to change. Is the mercy seat altered? Do the promises of God fail? Has God forgotten to be gracious? Will He be favorable no more? Even *"if we believe not, yet he abideth faithful: he cannot deny himself"* (2 Timothy 2:13). When everything else melts away, this one eternal Rock abides.

Therefore, *"my soul doth magnify the Lord, and my spirit hath rejoiced in God my Saviour."* It is a blessed string to touch. Take the time right now to play it and to evoke such harmonies that will make the angels want to join you in the chorus.

THE EIGHTH STRING OF GOD'S POWER

The next string that will awaken a responsive echo in your hearts is God's power: *"He hath showed strength with his arm; he hath scattered the proud in the imagination of their hearts."* This string gives us deep bass music and requires a heavy hand to make it pour forth any melody. What wonders of power God has produced on behalf of His people, from the days of Egypt, when He threw the horse and his rider into the Red Sea (Exodus 15:1), even until now! How strong is His arm to defend His people!

In these days some of us have been driven to look to that power, for all other help has failed. You know how it was in the Dark Ages: it seemed as if the darkness of popery could never be removed; but how soon it was gone when God called forth His men to bear witness to His Son! What reason we have to rejoice that He *"scattered the proud in the imagination of their hearts"!* They thought that they could readily burn up the heretics and put an end to this Gospel of theirs, but they could not do it. Even today there is a dark conspiracy to stamp out the evangelical faith on the part of some who promote their superstitions, set up the crucifix to hide the cross, and point men to sacraments instead of to the Savior. Worse than those are the people who undermine our faith in Holy Scripture, tear from the Book this chapter and that, deny this great truth or another, and try to bring the inventions of man into the place that ought to be occupied by the truth of God.

However, the Lord lives: Jehovah's arm has not waxed short (Numbers 11:23). Depend upon it, before many years have passed, He will take up the quarrel of His covenant and will bring the gospel banner to the forefront again. We will yet rejoice to hear the Good News preached in plainest terms, accentuated by the Holy Spirit Himself upon the hearts of His people.

Let us touch this string again. God Almighty, the Eternal One, is not dead. *"Behold, the LORD'S hand is not shortened, that it cannot save; neither his ear heavy, that it cannot hear"* (Isaiah 59:1).

THE NINTH STRING OF GOD'S SOVEREIGNTY

The next string is one that some friends do not like—at least, they do not say much about it. It is divine sovereignty. Listen to it. You know how God thunders it out. *"I will have mercy on whom I will have mercy, and I will have compassion on whom I will have compassion"* (Romans 9:15). God's will is supreme. Whatever the wills of men may be, God will not be driven from the throng, nor will His scepter be made to quiver in His hands. After all the rebellious acts of men and devils, He will still be eternal and supreme, with His kingdom ruling over all. Thus, Mary sang, *"He hath put down the mighty from their seats, and exalted them of low degree. He hath filled the hungry with good things; and the rich he hath sent empty away."*

Who can speak of the wonders of His sovereign grace? Was it not strange that He should ever have chosen you?

> What was there in you that could merit esteem,
>   Or give the Creator delight?
> "'Twas even so, Father," you ever must sing,
>   "Because it seemed good in Thy sight."

Do you think it is strange that the Lord should not take the kings and mighty ones, but should so order it that the poor have the Gospel preached to them? God is King of Kings and Lord of Lords, and He acts like a king. *"He giveth not account of any of his matters"* (Job 33:13). But He lets us see very clearly that He has no respect for the greatness and fancied goodness of man, that He does as He pleases, and that He chooses to give His mercy to those who fear Him and bow before Him. He dispenses His favors to those who tremble at His presence, who come humbly to His feet and take His mercy as a free gift; who look to His dear Son because they have nothing else to look to; and who, as poor, guilty worms, find in Christ their life, their wisdom, their righteousness, their all. Oh, the splendor of this great King!

THE TENTH STRING OF GOD'S FAITHFULNESS

The tenth string is God's faithfulness: *"He hath holpen his servant Israel, in remembrance of his mercy; as he spake to our fathers, to Abraham, and to his seed for ever."* God remembers what He has said. Take those three words, *"as he spake."* Whatever He said, though it was thousands of years ago, it stands fast forever and ever. God cannot lie.

Friends, are any of you in trouble? Search the Scriptures until you find a promise that suits your case, and when you find it, do not say, "I hope that this is true." That is an insult to God. Believe it, believe it up to the hilt. Do as I have seen boys do in the swimming pool: dive headfirst, and plunge right into the stream of God's mercy. Dive as deeply as you can. There is no drowning there. These are waters to swim in. The more you can lose yourself in this blessed crystal flood of promised mercy, the better it will be. You will rise up out of it as the sheep come from being washed. You will feel refreshed beyond measure in having cast yourself upon God.

When God's promises fail, let your pastor or your elders know of it. Some of us have lived so long on those promises that we do not care to live on anything else; and if they can be proved to be false, we had better give up living altogether. But, we delight to know that they are all absolutely true: what God said to our fathers stands good for their children, and it will stand good even to the end of time and to all eternity.

If any of you have not been able to touch even one of these strings, I would urge you get to your knees and cry out to God, "Why is it that I cannot magnify You, O Lord?" I should not be surprised if you discovered the reason to be that you are too big yourself. He who magnifies himself never magnifies God. Thus, belittle yourself, and greaten your God. Down with self to the lowest depths, and up—higher and still higher—with your thoughts of God.

Poor sinner, you who have not yet grasped the mercy and grace of God, there is sweet music even for you in Mary's song. Perhaps you are saying, "I am nothing but a lump of sin and a heap of misery." Very well, leave your pile of sin and your heap of misery, and let Christ be your All in All. Give yourself up to Christ. He is the Savior. Let Him do His business.

If I were being sued in court, I would not think of hiring an attorney to represent me, but then going into court and meddling with the case for myself. If I did, my attorney would say, "I must drop your case if you do not let it alone." Likewise, the idea may come into your mind that you will do something about saving yourself and have some share in the glory of your salvation. If you do not get rid of that idea, you will be forever lost. Surrender yourself to Christ, and let Him save you. Afterwards, He will work *"in you both to will and to do of his good pleasure"* (Philippians 2:13), while you make melody in your heart unto the Lord for all that He has done on your behalf. Then such delightful melodies will resound from your harp of ten strings that many will listen with such rapture that they will go to your Master and take lessons in this heavenly music for themselves.

The Lord bless you, beloved, and give you a grateful heart for all of His tender mercies to you!